# The Silent Struggle

**OrangeBooks Publication**

1st Floor, Rajhans Arcade, Mall Road, Kohka, Bhilai, Chhattisgarh 490020
Website: **www.orangebooks.in**

---



**First Edition, 2025**

**ISBN:** 978-93-6554-576-0

**Price:** Rs. 499.00



Printed in India

# The Silent Struggle

## Navigating Life after the Baby

Dr. Shraddha Sanghani

Orange Books Publication
www.orangebooks.in

# *Personal Note from the Author*

The inspiration for this book began the day I became a mother to my beautiful daughter. Like so many first-time moms, I was equal parts excited and overwhelmed. I had a thousand tabs open in my mind — and on my phone. I read everything I could get my hands on: articles, blogs, books, expert advice, mommy forums — you name it. I was determined to be ready, to be perfect, to have every possible checklist completed before she arrived.

But here's what I learned — and what I want to tell you, dear reader — you're more prepared than you think. The moment your baby comes into this world, something shifts. You won't feel instantly ready, but instinctively, you are. You don't need to become a walking encyclopaedia or a robotic version of the "ideal" mother. The truth is, the perfect mother already exists — within you. She's uniquely shaped for your child.

Every child is different. What works for one might not work for another. I remember my own mother gently telling me, "Don't try to force things on your baby. Keep trying, yes, but give her time to adjust. This is a whole new world for her, too." That advice became an anchor during the many moments when I felt unsure or when things weren't going as planned.

This book was born from the deep desire to reach out to new moms like me — those who want to do their best, who worry about the details, who try to prepare for everything, big and small. But motherhood isn't a test to ace. It's a journey to be lived. When we overthink every bump in the road, we lose the joy of the ride.

Motherhood will always come with its challenges, but what we don't always recognise is the incredible strength, intuition, and problem-solving ability we already possess. That gut feeling? That gentle inner voice? Trust it. It's real, and it's powerful. No one — not your doctor, your extended family, or the well-meaning neighbour auntie — knows your baby better than you do.

So let this book be your companion. Not a rulebook, but a friend. Not a checklist, but a warm hand on your shoulder, reminding you — you're doing okay. You don't have to be perfect. You just have to be present.

Let's walk this journey together, with honesty, compassion, and maybe a few laughs in between. You've got this. And I'm right here with you.

With love,

A doctor. A mother. And always, a fellow traveller.

# Table of Contents

## Chapter - 1

# The Real Beginning - What They Don't Tell You About Postpartum

"Congratulations! Your baby is here. Now you can rest and enjoy motherhood."

That's what everyone told me. I smiled, nodded, and even tried to believe it.

But let me be honest with you — as a doctor, I was prepared for labour, delivery, and neonatal care. What I wasn't fully prepared for was what came after: the physical exhaustion, the emotional whiplash, the loneliness even when surrounded by loved ones, the sore body, and the constant sense of "Am I doing this right?"

The real journey begins after childbirth — not just for your baby, but for you as a woman, as a mother, as a human being, healing and transforming.

This chapter is the one I wish someone had handed me in the hospital right after delivery. It's a summary of the most important things you must keep in mind and keep going back to it whenever you feel it's needed.

When we speak to new mothers, there's a phrase we hear time and again: "I'm tired. I'm stressed." But interestingly, when we dig deeper, the stress is rarely because of the baby. It's everything around the baby — the sleepless nights, the endless feeding worries, the constant second-guessing.

Is the baby sleeping enough? Eating enough? Gaining enough weight? Why does my friend's baby do things that mine doesn't? Why does her parenting style seem so effortless while I'm barely holding it together? There's the stress of low milk supply, the pressure of finances now that the mother may no longer be working, the guilt of leaving the baby behind if she is working and the discomfort of relying on grandparents and feeling like it's an obligation rather than a shared joy.

And yet, when we ask, "Do you ever regret becoming a mother?" — The answer is almost always a gentle, heartfelt "Never." Because even in the chaos, that one gummy smile, that tiny hand wrapping around your finger, the cooing, the cuddles — they make it all worth it. That little baby, who seems to create all the stress, is also the greatest stress-buster.

In the next few pages, I'll be sharing real stories from mothers — stories that echo your own, stories that remind you that you are not alone. Whatever you're going through is more common than you think. And yes— it will pass. And when it does, you'll see how all of it was shaping you into someone stronger, softer, and more deeply connected to the person you're becoming— a mother. This chapter is just a gist of most of the things you need to know about, and in the later chapters, we will discuss certain things in detail. So let's begin.

## *"Your Fourth Trimester: The Real Meaning of the 40-Day Rule"*

"Don't worry, beta, you'll be back to normal in 40 days," my well-meaning aunt told me after I had my daughter.

That number — *40 days* — gets thrown around a lot in Indian households, doesn't it? It's the magical timeframe for confinement, rest and healing. And yes, it's essential. But the reality? Your body doesn't work on a calendar.

My patient and friend Anitha, who had an emergency C-section, was still struggling to walk without pain after 6 weeks. Meanwhile, her cousin Priya, who had a vaginal delivery, was up and about in 10 days but faced relentless night sweats and mood swings for months.

Every woman's timeline is different — and there is no "normal." Your uterus might shrink back, but your energy, confidence, and hormone levels take much longer to stabilise.

### ❢ Take-Home Message:

*Postpartum recovery is not a one-size-fits-all process. Don't compare your healing journey with anyone else's— even your own previous delivery.*

However, let's understand a little more about the said "Confinement period."

The 40-day confinement period after delivery — known by various names in different cultures, such as "Jaappa" in North India or "Suaavad" time in Gujarat. It is rooted in ancient wisdom and modern science. It is a critical window for maternal recovery and infant bonding, and when understood and approached well, it can be deeply healing. However, many new mothers today find themselves dreading this period. The reason is that this period is imposed with rigid customs, isolation, dietary restrictions, and unsolicited advice that leave mothers feeling trapped, anxious, or even judged. However, this phase is not meant to be a punishment — it is nature's gift of recovery, and when embraced mindfully, it can be a nurturing and empowering experience.

## Why 40 Days Matter — Medically

**Hormonal Rebalancing:** After delivery, there is a steep drop in pregnancy hormones like progesterone and oestrogen. This hormonal crash is one reason mothers may feel weepy, irritable, or even anxious in the first few weeks. Rest and emotional support during this phase can help stabilise mood and prevent or reduce postpartum depression.

**Uterine Involution:** It takes about six weeks for the uterus to return to its pre-pregnancy size. During this time, vaginal bleeding (lochia) is common, and the cervix slowly closes. Avoiding physical strain or sexual activity during this period helps prevent infections and supports the healing of internal wounds, especially after vaginal delivery.

**Immunity Recovery:** Pregnancy suppresses the immune system to prevent the mother's body from rejecting the baby (a foreign body, genetically speaking). Post-delivery, the immune system starts to recalibrate. This makes mothers more vulnerable to infections in the initial days. Hence, the emphasis on hygiene, nutritious food, and staying warm during the confinement period isn't superstition — it's preventive medicine.

**Pelvic Floor and Muscular Recovery:** The pelvic floor muscles undergo significant strain during pregnancy and delivery. Rest, along with gentle movement and pelvic floor exercises when advised by a doctor, helps avoid long-term complications like incontinence or prolapse.

**Establishing Breastfeeding:** The early days are crucial for establishing a good breastfeeding routine. Skin-to-skin contact, unrestricted feeding, and a calm, distraction-free environment support both milk supply and the baby's latching ability. Having someone take care of chores while the mother focuses on this can make a huge difference.

### How Not to Make It Feel like a Punishment

**Personalise the Rituals:** Stick to the spirit, not the script. If traditional oils don't suit you, opt for lighter ones. If a particular food makes you feel bloated or uneasy, skip it. Don't blindly follow rules; modify them based on your comfort.

**Stay Connected:** Isolation leads to depression. Allow visits from people who uplift you — a friend who'll sit with you for chai, a cousin who makes you laugh, or a sister who gets you. You need support, not surveillance.

**Create a Cosy Nest:** Set up a comfortable corner in your room. Add soft lighting, soothing music, books, a rocking chair, or whatever brings you peace.

**Eat with Joy:** Postpartum food is meant to boost immunity and milk supply. Relish the ghee-laden laddoos or warm jeera water not as obligations, but as love — cooked with care, meant to heal.

**Communicate Boundaries:** It is okay to say, "I want quiet today," or "I'd like to hold my baby by myself now." You're allowed to set the tone of your recovery.

The 40-day confinement period is not a cage; it is a cocoon. It's a time when the mother, like her newborn, is fragile yet full of potential — a time when the body, mind, and identity are all recalibrating. Respect the science, embrace the emotion, and mould the tradition to support your healing, not stifle it. You don't have to "bounce back" — you're not a rubber band. You're a woman who just created life, and now it's time to pause, rest, and rise again — gently, joyfully, and on your own terms.

## *Your Body Is Not Broken, It's Healing*

When my friend Anjali delivered her second baby, I remember her saying, "I feel like I've been run over by a truck, but people expect me to walk like I just got a foot massage." I laughed, but only because it was so true.

The body after childbirth is a battlefield—tired, wounded, and desperately in need of rest and care. Yet somehow, we expect new mothers to be back on their feet, smiling in baby photos, and entertaining visitors within days.

Let me tell you what really happens behind the scenes of that glowing mother-baby selfie.

## The Inside Story: So Much Healing, So Little Talk

Your uterus, for starters, doesn't magically shrink back the moment the baby pops out. It takes around 6 weeks for it to return to its pre-pregnancy size. This process is called involution, and it's often accompanied by after pains — those mild cramps that feel like period pain. I remember my cousin Shruti calling me three days postpartum, whispering, "Why does it feel like early labour again?" No one had warned her about these little reminders of what her body was still going through.

If you've had a vaginal birth, your perineal area (the area between the vagina and anus) may have torn or been cut. Sitting, walking, and even laughing can feel painful in those early days. A friend once told me she was afraid to sneeze! For C-section moms, the pain is at the incision site — after all, it's major abdominal surgery. You've had multiple layers of tissue cut open and stitched back, and now you're expected to bend over, breastfeed, and change diapers.

## Your Core and Floor Need Help Too

No one tells you how fragile your pelvic floor is after delivery. These muscles have supported your baby for nine months and are stretched to their limits during labour. Many new moms experience urinary leakage (yes, peeing when you sneeze!) or a heavy feeling "down there." My friend Reema was terrified she'd done permanent damage until her doctor reassured her that with time — and the right exercises — she'd be fine.

Then there's diastasis recti, a gap that forms between your abdominal muscles during pregnancy. This often leads to the dreaded mommy pooch that won't go away with sit-ups (in fact, sit-ups make it worse!). You need specific core-strengthening moves, like guided physiotherapy or postpartum yoga, to help your body come back together — literally.

### Food, Sleep, and Love: Your Healing Trio

You're healing from blood loss, muscle strain, and fatigue, so eating well isn't a luxury — it's a necessity. Warm, nourishing foods like *panjiri*, *gond laddoos*, soups, dals, and iron-rich vegetables help replenish what your body has lost. In many Indian homes, grandmothers and mothers take over the kitchen to prepare these traditional postpartum foods.

Sleep, of course, is the most elusive part of healing. Newborns wake every 2–3 hours, and your own rest feels like a forgotten dream. Here's a tip: ask for help. If your mom, partner, or sister can watch the baby for just one uninterrupted nap, take it. One of my clients would hand the baby over to her husband at 6 am for one solid session of sleep — that was her golden hour.

### *The Emotional Side of Physical Healing*

Physical recovery can feel longer when you're mentally exhausted. When you're sore, leaking, and sleep-deprived, you start wondering, *"Is this what motherhood is going to be like forever?"* No, it won't be. But in the moment, it's okay to feel overwhelmed. You're not weak. You're healing.

#### Relatable Healing Moments

When your baby finally sleeps and you get 20 minutes to soak your feet in warm water — that's healing.

When your stitches don't sting as much while sitting — that's progress.

When you go from needing help to pee to walking to the kitchen on your own — that's winning.

When your breasts stop feeling like ticking time bombs— that's relief.

Healing is not an Instagram reel. It's slow, quiet, and deeply personal.

#### ❢ Take-Home Message:

*"Your body is not just recovering — it's reinventing itself."*

*Don't rush it. Don't compare it. And certainly, don't resent it. You've done the hardest job in the world. Now give your body the compassion, time, and patience it deserves. One day, you'll look back and admire your strength — not because you bounced back, but because you moved forward with grace.*

## The Emotional Aftershocks – More Than Just "Baby Blues"

I still remember sitting on my hospital bed, cradling my newborn daughter, and crying uncontrollably. Not out of pain, not even out of sadness — but this overwhelming wave of emotion that I couldn't quite explain. A nurse walked in, saw my tears, smiled gently and said, *"It's okay, sweetheart. The baby blues."* I nodded, but in my heart, I wasn't so sure.

Because what followed in the days and weeks after wasn't just fleeting weepiness. It was a whirlwind of self-doubt, guilt, fear, and isolation.

The time immediately after the delivery is a hormonal rollercoaster. After delivery, oestrogen and progesterone levels drop dramatically, which can make you feel moody, weepy, and even a little lost. Add to that the sleepless nights, leaking breasts, sore stitches, and you've got the perfect recipe for emotional overwhelm. One night, you're crying because your baby smiled; the next, you're crying because you spilt hot water. Both are valid.

### What Are the "Baby Blues"?

The "baby blues" are incredibly common — up to 80% of new mothers experience mood swings, irritability, anxiety, and crying spells in the first 2 weeks after delivery. It's mostly due to the sudden crash in oestrogen and progesterone levels post-birth. You've just gone through the biggest physical and emotional event of your life, and people expect you to feel "blessed"?

It's okay if you don't.

My friend Sonali, a first-time mom, told me, "I used to cry every evening around 7 pm. Nothing would be wrong, but I'd just fall apart. I thought something was wrong with me." It wasn't. That's the *baby blues*. They come like a wave and usually settle down within two weeks.

But what if it doesn't go away?

## When it's More Than Just Blues

If those feelings intensify, hang around longer than 2–3 weeks, or start affecting your ability to bond with your baby or take care of yourself, it might be *postpartum depression* (PPD). It's not rare. Around 1 in 7 mothers go through it, and many don't even realise it.

Shalini, a paediatric nurse I know, said she felt like a robot for the first two months after her baby was born. "I didn't feel love. I didn't feel joy. I just went through the motions." She finally opened up to her doctor, and with counselling and support, she slowly came out of that fog.

Some moms experience postpartum anxiety, constantly fearing that something terrible will happen to the baby. Others may feel intense rage or guilt. And in rare cases, there's postpartum psychosis, where a woman may lose touch with reality. That needs immediate medical help.

## Why Talking Helps

Most mothers don't speak up because they fear being judged. "You should be happy, not depressed," they're told. But emotions don't follow checklists. You're not a bad mother if you're struggling. You're a human mother.

Talk to someone — your partner, your doctor, a friend who's been there. Write in a journal. Join a new moms' support group. The weight often lessens just by saying, *"I'm not okay."*

💡 Take-Home Message:

*"It's okay not to be okay. But it's not okay to stay silent."*

*You are not alone. These emotional aftershocks are real, and they deserve real attention. Help exists. Healing happens. And joy does return — sometimes not in a rush, but quietly, like the baby's first real smile.*

### *The Silent Struggle – Loneliness and Identity Loss*

Motherhood has a strange way of making you feel lonely— even when you're never physically alone. Your house might be bustling with relatives, your phone may be flooded with "Congrats" messages, and yet, at 3 a.m., with a baby at your breast and everyone else asleep, the silence can feel deafening.

I still remember one such night, rocking Maanvi in the glow of a night lamp, hearing my husband snore peacefully beside me while my mother dozed in the next room. I wasn't angry at them — they were doing what they could — but the loneliness in that moment wrapped around me like a heavy blanket. It hit me: *No one else can be me right now. No one else can feel this particular exhaustion, this responsibility, this shift inside me.*

That's the strange part. You spend your whole life building an identity — maybe as a doctor, a teacher, a writer, a friend. And then suddenly, you're introduced as "Maanvi's mom." The world starts seeing you through the lens of motherhood alone. As beautiful and sacred as that role is, it often overshadows the person you were before.

Shalini, a driven marketing manager I had once spoken to, shared something similar. "Everyone keeps asking how the baby is sleeping or feeding," she said. "No one asks how *I* am. Honestly, I don't even know who I am anymore." She had gone from boardrooms to baby bottles, and the shift was jarring.

I suggested something simple: start journaling again — just 10 minutes a day. Shalini began writing letters to herself, processing the changes, grieving the parts she missed, and discovering new joys. "I feel like I'm talking to the old me," she told me after a few weeks. That ritual became her lifeline, her quiet way of reclaiming her sense of self.

Another friend, Aarti, used to love painting but hadn't touched a brush in months. One day, during her baby's nap, she pulled out her sketchbook and began with just a doodle. It wasn't a masterpiece, but it was hers. And that little act brought her back to herself in a way no amount of sleep could.

This isn't about rushing to "bounce back" or denying the beauty of your new role. It's about remembering that you matter too. Your dreams, your hobbies, your silly playlists, your coffee rituals — they're not selfish. They're *anchors*.

💡 Take-home message:

*It's normal to grieve the version of yourself that existed before motherhood.*

*But she's not lost — just layered beneath diapers, burp cloths, and lullabies. Start with one small ritual a day — write, stretch, paint, walk, sing in the shower. Bit by bit, you'll feel like you again — just with a deeper, more beautiful version of yourself in the making.*

### The Pressure to "Enjoy Every Moment"

Ah, this one. It hits you when you least expect it.

You're pacing the room with a crying baby who won't settle, your shirt is stained with milk, your eyes are burning from sleepless nights — and then someone says it:

"Enjoy every moment! These days are so precious!"

And you smile politely. But inside, you're thinking, really? Even this moment, where I feel like I'm falling apart?

We've all heard it. Well-meaning relatives, Instagram posts with dreamy baby photos, strangers at the doctor's clinic — they all offer the same advice. And while it comes from a place of love, it can be crushing. Because the truth is, not every moment of motherhood is enjoyable. Some moments are downright brutal.

I remember one night when I hadn't slept for more than 40 minutes at a stretch in over two days. Maanvi had colic, and the only thing that soothed her was me walking around carrying her. So I walked and sat cross - legged with her on me for hours. My back ached, my nipples were cracked from cluster feeding, and I had a bad fall from the numbness in my leg, which led to an ankle sprain. When someone texted me the next day, "These are the best days of your life! Soak them in," I nearly cried. If these are the best days, I thought, what does that say about the rest of my life?

Rekha, a mom I know who had just had her second child, shared something that stayed with me. She said, "The guilt of not enjoying motherhood was worse than the pain of childbirth." She felt like she was doing something terribly wrong just because she wasn't smiling through every diaper change or crying with joy every time her baby cooed.

I gently reminded her — and I remind every mother I meet — that you are not a bad mom for struggling. You are not broken. You are human. You are adjusting to an entirely new life, a new body, a new identity, and the 24/7 responsibility of another little human who can't tell you what they need. That's huge.

You're allowed to say, "This is hard."

You're allowed to cry.

You're allowed to not love every single second.

Motherhood is a mix of moments — some that melt your heart, others that test every ounce of your patience. And that's okay. You're not meant to enjoy every second; you're meant to live through them, as best as you can. Surviving some days is a win.

💡 Take-home message:

*Let go of the toxic positivity.*

*Not every moment of motherhood is magical — and that doesn't make you any less of a mother. The cracked, messy, sleep-deprived moments are just as real as the cuddles and baby giggles. And sometimes, just getting through the day is something to be proud of.*

### ***Social Media vs. Reality: What You See Isn't Always the Whole Story***

If you scroll through Instagram or Facebook as a new mom, you'll quickly notice a flood of picture-perfect moments. There are smiling babies in adorable matching outfits, moms showing off their "bounce-back" bodies just weeks after delivery, beautifully arranged nursery corners, and posts glowing with hashtags like #MomLifeIsBeautiful or #BlessedMom.

At first glance, it can seem like every mom is effortlessly managing motherhood with grace and style. But here's the truth many don't tell you: Behind those curated snapshots, many women are struggling — sometimes silently.

I remember talking to Neha, a mom who was visibly upset but hesitant to share her feelings at first. "On Instagram, all I see are these flawless moms," she told me. "I feel like I'm failing because my house is a mess, my baby won't stop crying, and I can't even find five minutes to brush my hair."

She confessed that she often found herself scrolling through endless posts late at night, only to feel more isolated and overwhelmed afterwards.

Or take Kavita, who shared that while her social media feed showed a happy family portrait, at home she was fighting painful mastitis and having frequent disagreements with her husband about how to share the parenting load. "Sometimes I cry alone in the bathroom because I'm exhausted and don't want anyone to see that side of me," she said.

These stories remind us: social media is a highlight reel, not the full movie. It's easy to forget that people post what they want the world to see — the carefully selected moments, the smiles, the triumphs — not the struggles, the tears, or the sleepless nights.

That's why I always encourage new moms to be mindful of what they consume online. Social media can be a wonderful place for support and inspiration — but only if it lifts you instead of tearing you down.

Here are some things you can do.

Follow accounts that make you feel seen and supported, not those that make you feel less than or ashamed. If a post or profile triggers self-doubt or comparison, don't hesitate to unfollow or mute.

Remember, your journey is unique. Someone else's "perfect" post doesn't mean your experience is any less valid or beautiful. You don't have to live up to someone else's highlight reel.

Seek out authentic voices. Moms who share the messy, real parts of motherhood — like sleepless nights, doubts, and struggles — can remind you that you're not alone.

Use social media intentionally. Limit your scrolling time and engage with communities that nourish your confidence and mental health.

As one of my patients wisely said, "I stopped chasing perfection online and started celebrating the small wins in my own life. Suddenly, motherhood felt less lonely."

💡 Take-home message:

*Curate your virtual village carefully. Surround yourself with stories and resources that nourish your confidence and celebrate your real, imperfect journey — not ones that erode your self-worth. Remember, behind every perfect photo is a real person with real struggles, just like you.*

📌 "Comparison is the thief of joy." — Theodore Roosevelt

### *The Role of the Care Team – Doctor, Doula, Dadi*

When a baby is born, so is a mother — and often, so is a whole village of helpers.

In India, postpartum care usually starts right at home — with mothers, mothers-in-law, grandmothers, and even helpful aunts jumping in with advice, food, massages, and constant checking in. It's a beautiful tradition — one that connects us to generations of women before us.

But let's be honest: sometimes, it can feel a bit overwhelming.

I remember Simi, a first-time mom who came to me looking tired, uncomfortable, and on the verge of tears. Her mother-in-law was doing what she believed was best: no bathing for 40 days, no fans, tight wrapping of the body in layers — even though it was peak summer in Hyderabad. Simi had developed a heat rash and was struggling to keep hydrated. But she didn't want to say anything at home for fear of sounding "ungrateful."

We had a gentle conversation, and I invited her mother-in-law to join. I explained the medical importance of hygiene and hydration and how those old customs had their place once, but needed to evolve with our times. Together, we found a middle path: Simi would bathe daily using lukewarm water, keep the fan on a low speed, and still enjoy traditional oil massages and nutritious home-cooked food. It was a respectful blend of tradition and science—and Simi finally looked relieved.

One important thing I always remind new moms is: you don't have to choose between culture and comfort—you can have both.

Let's also talk about the new grandparents — especially the new mom's own parents. Many women feel guilty asking their parents to move in or help out, worried they're "burdening" them. But the truth is, accepting help from your own mother, father, or siblings is not a sign of weakness — it's a natural, beautiful part of our culture. This is the same woman who once fed you when you were teething, soothed your fevers, and sat outside your exam hall for moral support. Why wouldn't she want to be there for you now?

Take Amrita's case. Her mother flew in from Delhi to help with her newborn in Bengaluru. Amrita hesitated at first — she didn't want her mom to feel pressured. But her mother told her, "Beta, I've waited my whole life to see you become a mother. Let me be here for you." That changed everything.

Your family — especially your own parents and siblings— aren't there out of duty. They're there out of love. Their support can be a lifeline in those exhausting early weeks, giving you space to recover physically and emotionally. Don't consider it as an obligation and embark on a guilt trip; rather, enjoy the bonding that develops between your child and her grandparents while you take a sigh of relief.

Don't forget the professionals in your care team. Your doctor, nurse, lactation consultant, or even a postpartum doula (if available) can offer medical support, guidance, and reassurance. They're trained to look out for complications, provide breastfeeding help, and make sure your recovery is on track. If you ever feel like family traditions are clashing with your well-being, these professionals can be your voice of reason — and backup.

At the heart of it all, you are the one healing, feeding, adjusting, and evolving. So you get the final say. Listen to advice, ask questions, take the help — but choose what feels right for you.

💡 Take-home message:

*Create a care circle that listens to your voice. Blend tradition with modern support. Your journey is your own— and you deserve to be at the centre of your postpartum care.*

📌 "Everyone wants to hold the baby. Make sure someone's holding the mother, too."

## Conclusion: Your Story Matters

Every woman's postpartum story is different, and all of them deserve to be told.

This chapter was not meant to scare you — but to prepare you. To normalise what has been hidden behind silence and shame for too long. We will be going back to a few of these topics in more detail in the coming chapters, which will help you get a deeper understanding of the core of the problems and some ways that you can handle them to have a beautiful and memorable postpartum period rather than a stressful and lonely one.

You are not alone. You are not inadequate. You are not "just being emotional."

You are going through one of the most transformative periods of your life — and you are doing it with strength, even if you don't feel strong every day.

Let's talk about it. Let's support each other. Let's rewrite the postpartum narrative together.

### 💡 *Final Take-Home Points:*

Postpartum recovery is messy, non-linear, and deeply personal.

Physical symptoms can take weeks to months to resolve— be patient and seek medical help when needed.

Mental health matters as much as physical health. Don't brush off persistent low moods.

You don't have to enjoy every moment to be a good mother.

You're not weak for needing help. In fact, asking for help is a sign of wisdom.

Your identity is allowed to evolve — you are more than "just a mom."

You deserve to be cared for, too.

This is the real beginning. Not perfect. Not polished. But powerful beyond words.

## Chapter - 2

# Recovery of the Physical Body after Delivery: Vaginal Birth and C–Section

The moment your baby is born, your world shifts. You're handed this beautiful bundle of joy, and with it, a tidal wave of emotions — love, joy, fear, exhaustion. Amidst the sleepless nights and the endless cycle of feeding and burping, there's another very real experience unfolding quietly: your body is healing.

Whether you've had a vaginal birth or a C-section, your body has been through a massive transformation. And while your baby becomes the centre of your world, it's vital not to forget that you matter too. That your healing matters. That your comfort, your strength, and your well-being deserve attention too. This chapter is for you—to guide you, support you, and walk with you through this journey of reclaiming your body.

## Vaginal Delivery: What Recovery Looks Like

For mothers who have had a vaginal delivery, the healing process can vary depending on several factors: whether you had a tear, an episiotomy, or an assisted delivery with forceps or vacuum. The first six weeks are usually the most intense.

### Common Issues Post Vaginal Delivery:

**Perineal pain:** This is from natural stretching or tearing during delivery, or from an episiotomy.

**Bleeding (lochia):** This is your body's way of shedding the lining of the uterus. It can last 4–6 weeks, starting heavy and gradually becoming lighter.

**Urinary incontinence or urgency:** Your pelvic floor muscles have been through a lot. You may experience a constant urge to pass urine, or discomfort while laughing and sneezing, and an inability to hold your pee.

**Haemorrhoids and constipation:** Straining during labour and the hormonal rollercoaster can make digestion sluggish, causing constipation. This leads to a medical condition called haemorrhoids, which may need medical assistance and sometimes surgical treatment. It can present as constant irritation in the anal region with or without pain, and can also sometimes make it even difficult to sit.

**Pelvic heaviness:** Some women describe it as feeling like "everything is about to fall out." This could be due to pelvic organ prolapse or weakened muscles.

I remember my cousin telling me in the hospital when I went to meet her "It's all swollen and sore down there." All I could tell her was its normal and that she could use some perineal spray or ointment and warm sitz bath, which may help her comfort the pain down there. My patient Aarti, a school teacher, confided in me how she cried every time she went to the bathroom for the first two weeks. She thought something was wrong until her mother-in-law reassured her that it was "normal."

It is normal — but that doesn't mean you should suffer silently. You can try Sitz bath – a tub with warm water and betadine and sit in it so that the water touches that area; or some ointments which help in numbing the pain for symptomatic relief.

### C-Section Recovery: A Major Surgery Deserves Major Care

A Caesarean section is a major surgical procedure. Let that sink in. You've just had abdominal surgery and now you're expected to care for a newborn round-the-clock.

I remember when Maanvi was in the ICU, I had to walk up to her to feed her; it was a task. Walking through the corridor to the ICU would bring tears of pain to my eyes. The first time I tried to get up and walk, I experienced the pain firsthand, and now I have more empathy for new mothers or any patients after a major procedure.

### Common C-Section Recovery Issues:

**Incision pain and numbness:** This can persist for weeks and even months. Some women experience a pulling sensation or numbness around the scar even months after the delivery.

**Gas and bloating:** The surgical process and limited mobility can slow down your gut, leading to a sense of fullness, indigestion and constipation.

**Difficulty moving:** Especially in the first week, getting out of bed or sitting up can be tough. Imagine an individual with a major abdominal surgery. The patient is made to rest for a minimum of 2 weeks in contrast to mothers who have to feed and care for a newborn. It is okay for you to complain of pain.

**Back pain:** Due to spinal anaesthesia, poor posture during breastfeeding, and weakened core muscles.

My cousin Neha had a C-section, and she told me she felt like she was "cut in half and stitched up again." She had no idea how long it would take to feel "normal" again. She struggled to lift her baby, and it took a physiotherapist and a supportive partner to help her navigate those first few weeks.

## Red Flags to Watch Out For

While discomfort and fatigue are expected, there are certain symptoms you shouldn't ignore. Here are some signs for which you need to reach out to your doctor:

Heavy bleeding: Soaking through more than one pad per hour or passing large clots.

Foul-smelling discharge: Could indicate infection.

High fever or chills: Especially in the first few weeks.

Severe pain not controlled by medication.

Redness, warmth, or pus from the C-section scar.

Leg swelling or pain (especially one-sided): Could be a sign of a blood clot.

Persistent sadness, hopelessness, or feeling unable to bond with your baby: These may be signs of postpartum depression.

A dear patient of mine, Lakshmi, ignored her fever and pain for a few days after her C-section because she didn't want to "bother anyone." When she finally came in, she had developed an infection that required hospitalisation. The gynaecologist referred her to me, and she was advised to take antibiotics for a few days, and then she recovered. I tell this to every new mother now: You are not a burden. Your health is important. Please address the early signs and symptoms and reach out for a medical consultation in person with your gynaecologist or physician at the earliest.

## What You Can Do To Support Recovery

**Rest:** Easier said than done, right? But every nap, every moment you can lie down and let your body recover, helps.

**Hydrate and eat well:** More on this in the nutrition section, but your body needs fuel to heal.

**Ask for help:** This is the time to lean on your village — whether it's your partner, your mom, or a hired helper.

**Pain relief:** Don't hesitate to take pain medications prescribed by your doctor. It doesn't make you look weaker or a lesser mother.

**Warm compresses or sitz baths:** Especially after a vaginal delivery, these can soothe soreness.

And most importantly, be kind to yourself. Healing doesn't happen overnight. You're not "bouncing back"— you're rebuilding. One day, one moment at a time.

## *Exercises Postpartum: Starting Slow, Building Strength*

The first time I tried to get out of bed after my C-section, I felt like my body had betrayed me. Muscles I didn't know existed screamed in protest. My core, which had once powered through long duty hours, loads of walking up and down and playing basketball and dancing, felt like jelly. I remember thinking, "Will I ever feel strong again?" Spoiler alert: yes, I did. But it didn't happen overnight.

If you've just delivered a baby — whether vaginally or via C-section — exercise is likely the last thing on your mind. And that's okay. But when the time is right, movement becomes not just a way to regain fitness but a crucial part of healing, mentally and physically. Exercising doesn't have to be always labelled or thought of as a part of your weight loss journey but more of an ingredient to fitness and recovering from the delivery.

### When Can I Start Exercising?

This is a question I get asked often during postpartum consultations. And rightly so. The short answer is: it depends. But there are general timelines that help as a guide.

For vaginal deliveries without complications, gentle movement can start within the first week. Things like breathing exercises, walking around your room, ankle rotations to improve circulation, and gentle stretches to prevent stiffness. For C-section moms like me, the body needs a little more time. Walking is encouraged from day one — just a few steps around your room with support — but anything involving core or lower body strength should wait until at least 6 weeks, and only after your doctor gives the green signal.

Most women are cleared for moderate exercise by 6-8 weeks postpartum, but that doesn't mean going back to your pre-pregnancy gym routine immediately. This is a time to listen to your body, not fight it.

## What Exercises Can I Do?

Let's break it down with a general week-wise plan that is gentle, realistic, and doable even with a newborn at home.

### Week 1-2:

Gentle walks around your room or balcony.

Deep breathing with belly expansion to engage your diaphragm and encourage abdominal activation.

Pelvic floor contractions (Kegels) — yes, these matter even after a C-section.

Shoulder rolls, neck stretches, and ankle pumps to ease tension and boost circulation.

### Week 3-5:

Gradually increase walking time to 10-15 minutes twice a day.

Add in gentle stretches — cat-cow, seated forward bends, side stretches.

Begin gentle core activation — not crunches! Think pelvic tilts while lying down.

### Week 6-8:

Once cleared by your doctor, you can start structured postpartum exercise programs.

Incorporate light strength training using body weight—squats, wall push-ups, and gentle resistance band exercises.

Introduce pelvic floor physiotherapy if needed.

Yoga tailored for postpartum women can be very beneficial, especially for spine and hip recovery.

### Week 8 onwards:

Gradually increase intensity and duration.

Start incorporating low-impact cardio like cycling, swimming, or dancing.

Work with a postpartum physiotherapist or certified trainer if you want to target specific goals like weight loss or core strengthening.

Remember, these are just broad timelines. Every woman's body is different. If you had complications, bleeding, or were advised to rest due to any medical reason, hold off and check in with your OB-GYN.

### What's the Deal with Diastasis Recti?

This term became quite popular on social media recently, but many moms still aren't sure what it really is. Diastasis recti is a separation of the abdominal muscles that occurs during pregnancy to accommodate the growing uterus. It's normal. But in some women, the separation doesn't close on its own and can lead to back pain, a poochy belly, and poor core strength.

You can check for it at home once your body feels ready:

Lie on your back, knees bent, feet flat.

Place one hand behind your head and gently lift your upper body.

Use your other hand to feel the gap between the two sides of your abdominal muscles above and below the navel.

If you can feel a separation wider than two fingers, it might be diastasis recti.

Don't panic. The good news is that with the right core exercises and physiotherapy, it can often be reversed. Avoid traditional ab exercises like crunches and sit-ups—they worsen it. Instead, focus on deep core activation techniques like:

Transverse abdominal breathing

Heel slides

Pelvic tilts

Modified planks (after 12 weeks or later)

Working with a physiotherapist who understands postpartum recovery makes a huge difference. My patient, Namrata, a 31-year-old mother, had a three-finger gap at six weeks postpartum. She started physiotherapy with targeted core work, and by 5 months, not only had her separation reduced, but her back pain had also disappeared. She told me, "I didn't know I had muscles there — but now I feel like I can stand tall again."

## The Importance of Massage and Relaxation

In our Indian culture, postpartum massage is almost a ritual. And rightly so. Done gently and with awareness, it helps in recovery and provides a moment to simply breathe.

Postpartum massage offers multiple medical benefits that support a mother's physical recovery after childbirth. It helps improve blood circulation, which in turn reduces swelling and accelerates the healing of tissues, especially in the lower back, hips, and abdominal area that bore the brunt of pregnancy and delivery. Massage also stimulates the lymphatic system, aiding in the removal of toxins and promoting better immune function. For mothers experiencing breastfeeding challenges, a gentle chest and upper back massage can relieve muscle tightness and improve milk flow. Additionally, massage reduces cortisol levels (the stress hormone) and boosts the release of oxytocin, promoting relaxation, better sleep, and emotional well-being — all crucial for a mother navigating the demands of a newborn.

Post-C-section moms should wait at least 2-3 weeks before starting gentle massage, and only if the scar is healing well. Use natural oils like coconut or sesame and work with a trained dai or physiotherapist. Scar massage, once advised by your doctor, can also reduce adhesions and numbness.

But physical relaxation isn't just about touch. Progressive muscle relaxation, deep breathing, yoga nidra, or even just lying down with soft music while the baby naps can recharge your system.

Take Shanvika, one of my patients from Hyderabad, who added 10 minutes of deep breathing and 5 minutes of journaling to her daily routine. "It felt silly at first," she admitted. "But I realised I was finally tuning into my own needs, not just my baby's."

## The Bigger Picture

Exercise during the postpartum period isn't about achieving a "flat stomach" or returning to your "pre-baby body" — it's about healing, rediscovering your strength, and reclaiming your sense of self. It's about moving again so you feel alive, not trapped in a body you don't recognise.

And it's completely fine to start small. Even five minutes of intentional movement can boost your mood. Some days, that five minutes may suffice. On other days, you might find your energy increasing, your spirit lifting, and before you realise it, you're doing ten. And then twenty.

You don't have to do this alone. Surround yourself with supportive people — whether it's a postpartum trainer, a friend who walks with you, or a group of new moms online sharing their daily wins.

Your body made life. Now, let it heal. Gently. Powerfully. On your own terms.

## Nutrition: Fuelling Your Recovery, Nourishing Your Baby, and Achieving Balance

After I delivered Maanvi, everyone from the hospital nurse to my mother to the neighbourhood auntie had a diet tip for me.

"Drink ajwain water daily, it melts the fat!"

"Don't eat cold foods or curd — your stitches will hurt more."

"Have ghee and laddoos, they'll give you strength."

Honestly, I was overwhelmed. I was healing from surgery, learning to breastfeed, sleeping in two-hour chunks, and now I had to worry about what was on my plate, too?

That's when I reminded myself of what I often tell my own patients: Postpartum nutrition is not about following fads or old wives' tales blindly. It's about balance — nourishing your recovering body and supporting your baby if you're breastfeeding, without adding pressure or guilt.

Let's walk through this together — what to eat, how to support milk supply, and yes, when and how to start losing that baby weight if that's your goal.

### The Basics: What Your Body Needs Postpartum

Whether you had a C-section or vaginal delivery, your body is healing from a major event. You've lost blood, stretched ligaments, used up nutrients, and now are possibly producing milk, which itself requires energy and resources. The goal of postpartum nutrition isn't to restrict or "bounce back," but to rebuild.

### Here's what your body needs most right now:

**Protein** – For tissue repair, hormone production, and supporting lactation.

💭 Dals, paneer, milk, curd, eggs, nuts, seeds, sprouts, tofu, lean meats if non-veg.

**Iron** – To rebuild blood levels and prevent postpartum anaemia (which is very common in Indian women).

💭 Green leafy vegetables, jaggery, dates, soaked raisins, garden cress seeds (haleem), red rice, and fortified cereals.

**Calcium** – For bone health, especially if breastfeeding (your baby takes calcium from your body).

💭 Dairy products, ragi (nachni), sesame seeds, almonds, leafy greens.

**Fibre** – To ease constipation, which many new moms struggle with post-delivery.

- Fruits, vegetables with skin, whole grains, oats, flaxseeds.

**Fluids** – Breastfeeding moms need extra hydration. Even otherwise, water helps with digestion, healing, and energy.

Drink at least 2.5 to 3 litres daily. Warm water is comforting, but there's no need to obsessively avoid cool water unless you feel unwell.

Tip from my experience: Keep a water bottle next to your feeding station. Sip while baby sips!

What to Eat to Support Milk Supply?

Now let's talk about lactogenic foods — foods traditionally believed to support breast milk production. While every mom is different and no one food guarantees more milk, many of these are nutritious and safe to try.

### Some great Indian lactation-friendly foods

Fenugreek (methi) – Add to dal or drink as tea

Fennel seeds (saunf) – Soaked overnight or in tea

Garden cress seeds (haleem/alikira) – High in iron and good for milk

Shatavari powder – An Ayurvedic herb often prescribed for milk supply (only under medical guidance)

Coconut and coconut water – Hydrating and energising

Garlic – A common ingredient in postpartum food, believed to enhance milk and digestion

And yes, gond ke laddoo, ajwain paratha, daliya, halim water — these all have their place when made thoughtfully, not dripping in excess ghee or sugar. A little indulgence is part of healing.

Just remember — if you're breastfeeding and still feel your supply is low, it's not just about diet. It's also about frequent nursing, the baby's latch, hydration, and rest. Don't hesitate to reach out to a lactation consultant for help.

## Postpartum Dieting – When and How to Start Weight Loss

Let's get this out of the way — you do NOT need to go on a diet right after delivery. Your body needs nourishment, not deprivation. For the first 8-12 weeks, your focus should be on healing, milk supply (if nursing), and stabilising hormones.

But I understand the reality — many of us feel bloated, heavier, and not ourselves. There's pressure (external and internal) to "get back in shape."

Here's how to approach postpartum weight loss with kindness:

### Start Only When:

Your energy levels are stable

You're sleeping at least 4-5 hours in 24 hours (even broken sleep)

You've seen your doctor for a postpartum check

Your milk supply is well-established

Usually, around 12–16 weeks postpartum is a safe time to begin structured dietary changes — emphasis on structured, not crash diets!

### How to Begin:

Cut down on empty calories: sugar-loaded biscuits, fried snacks, soda.

Keep meals frequent and small: aim for 3 major and 2 mini meals.

Balance each meal with protein + fibre + healthy fat.

Don't skip carbs — choose smart ones: red rice, whole wheat roti, millets, wheat/multigrain bread.

Use portion control instead of food elimination.

Once you have control over yourself about the food you should not be eating and are able to control your cravings, you could try stricter diet regimens for faster results. However, refrain from intermittent fasting and FAD diet regimens when you are still nursing your baby.

Sample Diet Plans for Different Stages

These are eggetarian, realistic Indian options that can be customised further.

| Time | Week 1–4 (Healing Focus) | Week 5–12 (Energy + Milk Supply) | Week 12+ (Weight Loss & Strengthening) |
|---|---|---|---|
| **Morning** | Ajwain water + soaked almonds | Jeera water + nuts & seeds mix | Lemon water + handful of walnuts |
| **Breakfast** | Dalia with ghee + dates | Vegetable upma + curd | Boiled eggs or tofu + multigrain toast |
| **Mid-morning** | Fruit (banana or papaya) + coconut water | Buttermilk + fruit | Cucumber + carrot sticks with hummus |
| **Lunch** | Rice + moong dal + lauki sabzi + beetroot + ghee | Brown rice + chana dal + bhindi + salad | Roti + rajma + stir-fried vegetables |
| **Snack** | Gond laddoo or ragi porridge | Sprouts chaat or peanut sundal | Greek yoghurt + fruit |
| **Dinner** | Roti + paneer bhurji + spinach soup | Roti + dal + methi sabzi | Quinoa or millet khichdi + sautéed greens |
| **Bedtime** | Warm turmeric milk | Halim seeds in warm milk | Chamomile tea or haldi milk |

## Real Stories: Food can make you feel better

*Rucha*, a 33-year-old software engineer, felt “flabby and fatigued” after her delivery. She wasn’t producing enough milk and started panicking. On evaluation, she had low iron and was eating just toast and tea twice a day. We built a simple food routine around her baby's sleep cycle and added nutrient-rich foods like halim seeds, soaked dates, palak dal, and jaggery-based snacks. Not only did her energy pick up, but so did her supply.

Sarika, a 33-year-old mother, after 3 months of delivery, started doing her dieting, which she had done earlier in her pre-marriage dates. She not only felt like failing because she was not losing any weight, but also had very low energy levels and frequent emotional breakdowns. I told her to just eat whatever she wants without feeling guilty to begin with, then slowly removed the empty calories and made her understand clean eating techniques. In just 6 months, she was way better, sometimes even indulging in chocolates and pastries with no guilt and a healthier physique.

Priyanka, a new mom, was overwhelmed with weight gain. She kept skipping meals and then bingeing out of hunger. We focused on consistency — not restriction. Within 3 months of regular meals, home workouts, and patience, she had shed the guilt first — and then the kilos.

Consistency in Diet and exercise is the key. Don’t aim for bouncing back, and don’t put a target date. Slow and steady truly will help you gain your strength and curate a new and healthier version of yourself.

### Nourish, Don't Punish

Food should be your friend in this journey. Not a burden. Not a battleground.

If you're hungry all the time, it doesn't mean you have no willpower — it probably means your body needs more of the right things.

If you're not losing weight quickly, it doesn't mean you're failing — it means your body is healing at its own pace.

Your baby is growing from the food you eat. But you, too, are growing into a new version of yourself. You deserve to be fed, fuelled, and cared for with love.

### *Gaining Back Confidence – Rediscovering the 'You' in Mom*

I remember looking in the mirror one afternoon when Maanvi was around two months old. My body was softer, my eyes had dark circles, and my favourite kurti from before pregnancy didn't fit quite right anymore. My first instinct was to sigh and walk away. But then I paused.

"This body made a whole human being," I whispered to my reflection. "It deserves love, not judgment." That day we went out shopping and I bought myself new clothes. That made me feel so nice, and the small gesture I did helped me gain confidence in the new "me" I was carving myself into.

Rebuilding confidence after having a baby isn't about fitting into your pre-pregnancy jeans or getting compliments from others. It's about how you feel when you look at yourself. It's about slowly, steadily reclaiming ownership over your time, space, identity — and your body.

This chapter isn't about giving you a makeover plan. It's about helping you see your new self with kindness, and permitting yourself to bloom again — this time, with deeper roots.

### 1. Appreciate Your New You

It's easy to mourn the old you. The carefree girl who didn't carry leaking breast pads or schedule her day around nap windows. But what if you celebrated the new you instead?

You are stronger now — not just physically, but emotionally.

You are more empathetic, more capable, more resilient than ever.

You've learned the art of waking up at 3 am and functioning with one hand (and half a brain cell).

Take a moment. Look at yourself. And say it out loud: "I'm proud of me."

That's not arrogance — it's healing.

***"You're not who you were before, but that doesn't mean you've lost yourself. You've expanded."***

**— Unknown**

Ritu, a teacher from Delhi, told me she wrote daily affirmations on her bathroom mirror after childbirth.

"Some days I believed them, some days I didn't. But I still wrote them."

Try it. One kind word to yourself every day.

**2. Get Dressed, Even If You're at Home**

It might seem superficial, but what you wear can impact how you feel. No, I'm not asking you to wear jeans or lipstick if that feels like too much. But changing out of the feeding-stained nightie, brushing your hair, and wearing a fresh kurta can do wonders.

**It tells your brain:** I matter. I am showing up for myself today.

My patient Ananya started wearing simple jhumkas and putting on her favourite perfume at home, even while caring for her twins. "I felt more human," she said. "Not just like a milk machine."

Dress in a way that reflects you beyond the diapers and burp cloths.

Another mother, Harika, a mother of a one-year-old called me for a consultation, saying she was not just able to cope. After discussing her daily routine (which wasn't there), I made her make some small changes and added a compulsory getting-ready time in the morning and freshening up in the evening. She said reluctantly," It is not going to work." I requested her to try it for 2 weeks and then get back to me. To my surprise, the small change not only uplifted her mood, but she was also able to make a proper routine for herself and her child and felt as if she had ample time left for herself.

Body confidence doesn't come from the mirror alone. It comes from movement, mindfulness, and self-compassion. For many mothers, social media adds pressure. Perfect bodies, flat stomachs in 30 days, "bounce back" stories — it's overwhelming.

Tanvi, a mom blogger, told me, "Every time I opened Instagram, I felt like a failure. Everyone seemed to have it together but me." She eventually took a break, followed body-positive accounts, and started journaling. "I began to see the value in my body's journey, not its size," she said.

💡 Take-home message:

*Unfollow what makes you feel less. Follow what empowers you.*

*This isn't about impressing others — it's about sending signals to your own self-esteem that you're alive, vibrant, and present.*

**3. Make a Routine and Stick to It**

There's chaos in those early months. But creating even a basic routine helps you feel in control. And in that routine, carve out 15-30 minutes daily just for you.

Whether it's:

A solo chai on the balcony

A walk with your favourite podcast

Journaling or prayer

Reading one chapter of a book

Schedule it like it's a doctor's appointment. Because it is—a prescription for your sanity.

My personal tip? I started setting a reminder, "Maanvi sleeps, Mama breathes" during her afternoon nap. It became my sacred pause, where I could think and do the things I always wanted to do but couldn't because of my busy work schedule.

Making a routine is not only good for you, but it also instils discipline in your child and the importance of following a schedule. Working around a timely routine might seem boring and monotonous, but in the chaos that is only going to increase as your child grows, that boring schedule will become your anchor, something you can look back at when you are clueless as to where to begin.

### 4. Spend Quality Time with Yourself

Remember the version of you before motherhood? What did she love to do?

Dance?

Sketch?

Bake?

Learn languages?

Do yoga?

She's still in there. Not gone — just waiting to be invited back.

Don't fall into the trap of feeling selfish for prioritising yourself. Your child benefits from a mother who feels fulfilled, not one who's constantly depleted.

Bhavna, a new mom, told me she rejoined her online Kathak class 4 months after her C-section. "I felt guilty at first, but after the first few beats, I cried. I had missed me."

Reclaiming your body is not just physical. It's emotional, spiritual, and deeply personal.

## Conclusion: You Are Not Lost, You're Becoming

You may not feel like yourself yet. That's okay.

But trust me — she's in there. She's watching. She's waiting.

And each nourishing meal, each gentle stretch, each moment of rest, each smile in the mirror is a breadcrumb leading her back home.

Motherhood doesn't erase you. It expands you.

So take your time.

Reclaim your body, your rhythm, your spark — on your terms.

And remember, even when it feels like you're unravelling — you are actually being rewoven into something strong.

***"Rest is not a luxury in motherhood. It is recovery."***

**— Dr. Shraddha**

***"You did not lose yourself in motherhood. You gave birth to a new version."***

**— Dr. Shraddha**

## Chapter - 3

# Emotional Earthquakes - Understanding Postpartum Depression and Baby Blues

The mental health of new mothers is a topic that often remains tucked away behind baby photos and congratulations. Yet, it's as real and important as physical recovery. When a baby is born, so is a mother. And just like the baby needs nurturing and care, so does the mother — especially emotionally. The postpartum phase is not only about feeding, swaddling, and burping. It's also about dealing with anxiety, doubt, fear, guilt, and sometimes, overwhelming sadness.

There's a moment in those first few days after childbirth that many women will never forget. It's the moment when you hold your baby in your arms, but instead of being overwhelmed with joy, you're overwhelmed with tears — and not the happy kind. It's a strange place to be, especially when everyone around expects you to be glowing, smiling, grateful. But inside, you might feel hollow, confused, even a little bit scared. You're not ungrateful. You're not a bad mother. You're human — and you've just gone through one of the biggest emotional earthquakes your mind and body will ever experience.

Let's start with the science of it all — hormones. During pregnancy, your body is swimming in hormones like oestrogen and progesterone, which help sustain the pregnancy and keep your mood relatively stable. But right after delivery, those hormone levels drop dramatically, almost like a cliff fall. This sudden shift can send your emotional balance into a spin. Add to that the stress of sleepless nights, breastfeeding struggles, pain from healing stitches or surgical wounds, and the responsibility of keeping a tiny human alive — and it's no wonder that many mothers feel like they're on the verge of falling apart.

Ritika, a cheerful HR professional, was known for her sunny smile. She gave birth to her daughter with caesarean section and was surrounded by family and friends. But within a week, she found herself crying in the middle of the night, unable to sleep even when the baby was asleep. "Everyone told me I was lucky," she said. "I had a healthy baby, good support at home, and yet I couldn't stop feeling like something was broken inside me. I felt like I was drowning, but didn't know how to ask for help." Ritika was experiencing what we call the "baby blues."

Baby blues are incredibly common — affecting nearly 70 to 80 per cent of new mothers. They usually show up within the first few days after delivery and can include: Frequent crying spells, Mood swings, Irritability, Anxiety, Feeling overwhelmed and Difficulty sleeping (even when the baby sleeps).

The good news? They tend to resolve on their own within two weeks. The key during this time is rest, reassurance, support, and time. Partners, family members, and caregivers need to understand that this phase is not attention-seeking or weakness — it's biology.

But sometimes, those blues don't go away. They linger, deepen, and start affecting your ability to function. That's when we start talking about postpartum depression (PPD) — a real, diagnosable mental health condition. PPD is not a character flaw. It is not something you can snap out of. It is not solved by simply "thinking positively." It's a complex interplay of biological, emotional, and social factors, and it needs to be taken seriously.

Madhavi, a school teacher, shared that her postpartum depression crept in like a fog. "I was okay for the first couple of weeks," she said. "Then one day, I looked at my baby and felt nothing. No love, no joy. Just emptiness. I thought I was a monster." She started withdrawing from her family, stopped eating properly, and began having thoughts that scared her. Her husband noticed the change and gently insisted she talk to a counsellor. With therapy and support, Madhavi slowly found her way back.

### PPD can manifest in different ways:

Persistent sadness or low mood

Loss of interest in things you once enjoyed

Feeling disconnected from the baby or having difficulty bonding

Low energy or constant fatigue

Difficulty concentrating or making decisions

Appetite changes (eating too much or too little)

Feeling guilty, hopeless, or worthless

Sleep Problems

Thoughts of self-harm or harming the baby (in severe cases)

It can begin anytime in the first year after childbirth, not just immediately after delivery. The most important thing to remember is that if these feelings last more than two weeks or interfere with daily life, it's time to seek help.

In rare but severe cases, mothers may experience postpartum psychosis — a psychiatric emergency. This can involve

Hallucinations (hearing voices, seeing things)

Delusions (irrational or paranoid thoughts)

Extreme confusion or disorientation

Agitation or restlessness

Mania or rapid speech

Thoughts of harming self or baby

It usually begins within the first few weeks after childbirth and requires immediate medical intervention. While it's rare (affecting about 1 in 1000 women), it's important to know the signs so that swift action can be taken.

## Common Causes of Postpartum Depression in Indian Mothers

### Lack of Emotional Support or Understanding

Aparna, a new mom, felt isolated in her joint family. Despite help with chores, no one seemed to understand her need for rest or her struggles with breastfeeding. "They kept saying, 'we all did this, why are you crying?'" she recalled. The constant invalidation made her feel guilty and alone.

### Sleep Deprivation

Interrupted sleep for weeks on end can make even basic thinking difficult. Without restorative rest, mood swings and irrational thoughts become common.

### Unrealistic Expectations and Pressure to Be "Perfect"

Zainab, a first-time mother from Hyderabad, constantly compared herself to social media influencers. "Everyone looked so happy and thin. I felt like I was the only one failing."

### Difficult Childbirth or Birth Trauma

Emergency C-sections, NICU admissions, or unplanned outcomes can be traumatic and leave a lasting emotional impact.

### Previous History of Depression or Anxiety

Women with a history of mood disorders are more prone to experiencing postpartum depression.

### Physical Pain and Complications

Lingering pain from stitches, haemorrhoids, breast engorgement, or infection can affect both mood and energy levels.

### Gender Bias and Societal Expectations

In some families, the pressure to have a male child still exists, or there's criticism if a woman chooses not to breastfeed or returns to work soon after childbirth. This can lead to feelings of guilt and inadequacy.

Mental health is just as vital as physical health. Just like we would never ignore a high fever or heavy bleeding after childbirth, we should never ignore persistent emotional distress. The challenge is that mental health doesn't always have visible signs. You might be wearing clean clothes, feeding your baby, and even managing to smile at visitors — but inside, you might be falling apart. This is why awareness and open conversations are so essential.

Sometimes, the first step to healing is simply being heard.

It's a strange place to be in — when your world is supposed to be overflowing with joy, but all you can feel is an overwhelming sense of emptiness, fear, or even rage. You're holding a baby, your own child, and yet the connection doesn't come instantly. You might feel numb, unsure, or secretly disappointed in yourself. You might cry without knowing why, lash out at people you love, or retreat into yourself. And the guilt — oh, the guilt of feeling like this when everyone expects you to be happy — can be soul-crushing.

But here's the truth no one tells you loud enough: it's not your fault. And you are not alone.

One of the key aspects of dealing with postpartum depression is to recognise that it's not a reflection of how much you love your baby or how good a mother you are. It's a medical condition, influenced heavily by hormonal changes, physical exhaustion, emotional overload, and often, social isolation. Let's not forget the cultural expectations we often carry in India — being a "sanskaari" daughter-in-law, keeping the home perfect, hosting relatives, smiling politely through rituals, even when your body and mind are barely keeping up.

Take, for instance, Priya, a 29-year-old new mother. She was well-educated, had a supportive husband, and a much-wanted pregnancy. But after delivery, she began to feel like a shadow of herself. Every morning felt like a mountain. She couldn't stop crying, avoided feeding the baby out of anxiety, and felt convinced she was failing. Her mother-in-law brushed it off as "nazar lag gayi," and her mother said, "Ye toh sabko hota hai. Adjust kar lo."

It wasn't until her husband insisted they see a counsellor that she was diagnosed with moderate postpartum depression. With medication and therapy, she slowly began to feel like herself again.

That intervention saved her months, possibly years, of silent suffering.

Seeking medical help isn't weakness — it's wisdom. There are psychiatrists and therapists who specialise in perinatal and postpartum mental health. In many cases, especially with moderate to severe symptoms, therapy may be combined with medications that are safe even during breastfeeding. What's important is consistent follow-up, because healing isn't linear. There might be good weeks and bad ones — but with help, you'll notice a steady upward curve.

Now, let's talk about support systems. They're everything. One of the most underappreciated pillars of postpartum mental health is the partner. When a husband is tuned in — emotionally available, involved in daily care of the baby, and willing to shoulder home responsibilities — it creates a sense of safety and shared burden. A simple, "You're doing great, I'm proud of you," said genuinely, can make the difference between a woman feeling completely alone and completely supported.

Then there are friends. Remember those long, comforting chats before baby came along? You need them now more than ever. It may feel awkward at first to reach out and say, "I'm not okay." But you'll be surprised how many other moms have felt the same. It's in these candid conversations that healing begins. Support groups — whether local mom circles or online forums — offer that sense of "me too" that can be powerfully validating. We will discuss more in the chapter "You are not alone".

Also, journaling. A small notebook by the bedside where you can pour your thoughts out — raw, messy, real. There's something liberating about writing down fears you can't yet say aloud. It's like unclogging a blocked drain — suddenly, emotions begin to flow again.

I remember, I used to get very angry and lose my mind at my husband so often that I felt sorry for him. To reduce my outbursts I kept a diary in my clinic and started writing in it as if I was talking to him or my parents. I then realised that out of 100 complaints I may have had, 10 would be actually something I needed to talk about. This helped me become calmer and express the real issues rather than just bombarding the poor soul with my emotions.

And sometimes, what you need is simply silence. A short walk. Ten minutes of deep breathing. A solo coffee. A long shower. These tiny rituals of solitude can bring immense grounding when everything else feels chaotic.

Another helpful tool? Task stratification. Many new moms are overwhelmed not because of the baby, but because of all the peripheral responsibilities they're expected to shoulder. From hosting guests to managing bills to resuming work emails, everything demands attention. But everything doesn't deserve it. Learn to categorise:

> **Important and Urgent** – e.g. feeding the baby, visiting the paediatrician.
>
> **Important but Not Urgent** – e.g. scheduling your postpartum check-up, renewing health insurance.
>
> **Urgent but Not Important** – e.g. replying to that WhatsApp family group message.
>
> **Not Important and Not Urgent** – e.g. folding laundry to perfection.

Stick to doing categories 1 and 2. Delegate or delete categories 3 and 4. This simple mental exercise can help you reclaim hours of mental space.

It's also time we, as a society, normalise saying "no." You don't have to say yes to visitors just because they came with gifts. You don't have to cook a three-course meal or attend a naming ceremony two weeks postpartum. You don't even have to pick up every phone call. Your health — mental and physical — takes priority. That's not selfish, that's survival.

Sunita, a 33-year-old mother of twins from Hyderabad, shared how she created a "do-not-disturb" zone for herself between 1 and 2 p.m. daily. Everyone in the household, including her in-laws, knew this was her sacred hour. Sometimes she slept, sometimes she meditated, sometimes she just lay there. That one hour gave her the sanity to handle the other twenty-three. Boundaries aren't rude — they're essential.

Let's also remember that hormones continue to fluctuate for months, sometimes even a year postpartum. Estrogen and progesterone, the key pregnancy hormones, drop suddenly after birth. Oxytocin, the love hormone, spikes with skin-to-skin and breastfeeding but can be easily disrupted by stress. Cortisol, the stress hormone, may remain elevated if sleep is poor or emotional support is missing. All of this creates a hormonal cocktail that can either nourish or destabilise mental health, depending on the woman's overall ecosystem.

That's why lifestyle adjustments play a huge role in mood regulation.

Prioritise sleep — if not 7 hours at a stretch, then 2-3 hours in cycles.

Eat well — complex carbs, good fats, proteins, and lots of water.

Move your body, even if it's just gentle stretching or a short walk in sunlight. These may sound basic, but they are the foundation.

Above all, extend compassion to yourself. Be gentle. This isn't the time to expect productivity or perfection. It's a time of survival, of raw beauty, of imperfection, and of courage.

A quote I often share with new moms is by Nora Ephron: "Be the heroine of your life, not the victim." And sometimes, being the heroine means asking for help, drawing boundaries, crying when you need to, and laughing when you can.

Because no matter what the glossy pictures or baby albums show, motherhood is messy. It's vulnerable and intense and breathtaking and exhausting, all at once.

But you, dear mother, are doing better than you think. And you are not alone.

## What about Him? Postpartum Mental Health in Fathers

We talk so much — and rightly so — about the mother's emotional journey after childbirth. But in doing that, we often forget there's someone else quietly transitioning into parenthood too. The father. His clothes haven't changed sizes. He didn't physically push a baby out. He may have even returned to work within a week or two. But emotionally? Everything's changed.

We rarely stop to ask new dads, *"Are you doing okay?"* The spotlight is on the mother and the baby, and the father is expected to quietly carry on. But just like mothers, fathers too experience emotional upheaval, self-doubt, and even depression during the postpartum period.

Let me tell you about Anirudh. He was that eager, loving, involved partner during Shruti's pregnancy — attending all the Lamaze classes, painting the nursery walls pale yellow, and learning how to hold a newborn on YouTube. But when their daughter was born, everything suddenly became about Shruti and the baby (understandably so), and Anirudh found himself fumbling in the dark — unsure of how to help, how to bond with the baby, or even what his role was now. One night, after failing to console the baby and accidentally waking Shruti, he sat in the kitchen with his head in his hands and whispered, “I feel like I’m not needed.”

This is more common than we think. Studies show that up to 10% of new fathers experience postpartum depression — and those are just the reported cases. Many more go unspoken and unacknowledged. Because men are often conditioned to be “strong,” many new dads suppress their feelings, throw themselves into work, or numb their stress with screen time or alcohol, instead of reaching out for help.

Their emotional struggles might not look like the classic image of depression. Instead of crying or expressing sadness, they may become irritable, withdrawn, or distracted. They might feel overwhelmed, anxious about finances, insecure about parenting, or unsure of how to support their partner.

Karan, another father I spoke to, said: “She was breastfeeding and bonding with the baby. I felt like an outsider… like my only job was to hold the fort, but not be part of the magic.”

Many fathers silently carry anxiety about leaving the newborn and partner at home as they return to work — grappling with guilt over not being present enough, and helplessness when they can’t contribute to daily caregiving as much as they would like. For some, especially when the mother and baby are at the maternal home, there’s a growing sense of emotional distance. The early bonding moments they long for often feel out of reach, replaced by photos and video calls. Add to that the mixed messages from society: if he’s not seen changing diapers or missing work for his newborn, he's labelled uninvolved. But if he does participate equally, he's praised like he's gone above and beyond — something mothers are never applauded for. These conflicting expectations can leave fathers feeling judged no matter what they do. It's time we acknowledge that just like mothers, fathers, too, need support, space, and validation in this new role. A kind word, involvement in decision-making and conscious inclusion by the mother can go a long way in helping fathers feel connected and confident.

So what can mothers do to support fathers through this emotional transition and help them feel included in parenting?

### Here are a few things that truly help:

#### Acknowledge his feelings.

Ask him, "How are you doing?" and mean it. Listen without immediately jumping in with solutions. Sometimes just being asked and heard is healing.

#### Share responsibilities, even if imperfect.

Let him change diapers, bathe the baby, or take the baby for a walk — even if he doesn't do it exactly like you would. Dads bond through doing, not just watching.

#### Involve him in feeding routines.

If you're breastfeeding, he can bring the baby, burp them afterwards, or sit beside you and talk. If you're pumping or using formula, let him take over some feedings. These moments can help him feel connected.

### Encourage solo dad time.

It might be tempting to hover, but trust him to handle a 20-minute cuddle session or a diaper change without supervision. Let him find his own rhythm with the baby.

### Appreciate and affirm.

A simple, "You're such a good dad", can go a long way in boosting his confidence. New fathers need validation just like new mothers do.

### Make space for a couple times.

Amidst feeding, burping, and naps, try to find small pockets of time to reconnect as a couple. A 15-minute walk, a shared coffee, or even lying down and holding hands can remind both of you that you're still a team.

### Encourage him to talk to friends or professionals.

Sometimes, men find it easier to open up to a friend or a counsellor. Gently suggesting this as an option can be a loving nudge in the right direction.

Remember, just like mothers, fathers too are adjusting to a completely new role, with high expectations and very little guidance. Some may be struggling with financial stress, job pressure, or guilt for not being home more. Others may feel sidelined or invisible during this phase, especially if all the attention is on the mother-baby duo.

And if you, as a mother, are going through your own emotional storm (which is completely valid), it may feel impossible to look out for someone else. But think of it this way — when both partners feel seen, supported, and emotionally well, the entire family thrives.

As Mansi, a new mother of twins, shared with me: "We were both sleep-deprived, cranky, and clueless. But the night I saw him crying silently after rocking both babies for an hour… I realised he was struggling too. I hugged him and said, 'We're doing this together.' That moment changed everything."

### Take-home message:

*Parenthood is not just about the baby. It's about both of you. The mother and the father. Each carrying emotional weight, each needing rest, support, and love. Let's normalise asking fathers how they feel. Let's make space for their emotional health too. Because when the whole family is cared for, the baby gets the most secure, loving environment to grow up in*

### Summarizing

Your mental health matters — just as much as your baby's physical health. If you're feeling low, overwhelmed, anxious, or detached, know that it's not a sign of weakness or failure. It's a sign to pause and check in with yourself.

Hormonal changes after delivery are real and powerful. The sudden drop in estrogen and progesterone, combined with sleep deprivation and emotional upheaval, can deeply affect your mood and thoughts. It's not 'just in your head' — it's happening in your body too.

Postpartum blues are common and usually resolve within 2 weeks. But if your symptoms persist, worsen, or interfere with your ability to function or bond with your baby, it might be postpartum depression — and you deserve support.

**Red flags that need attention include:**

- Persistent sadness, hopelessness, or numbness
- Loss of interest in things you once enjoyed
- Difficulty bonding with your baby
- Thoughts of harming yourself or your baby
- Feeling like a bad mother or that your family is better off without you

These are not signs of failure. They are signs you need help — and help is available.

You are not alone. Many mothers go through this. Sharing your feelings with a friend, family member, or professional can make a world of difference. Seek out support groups — online or offline. Let others walk with you.

Your partner's support is crucial – both ways. A listening ear, shared responsibilities, and consistent encouragement from your spouse or family members can be a powerful buffer against depression.

Counselling and therapy work. Don't hesitate to speak to a trained mental health professional. For moderate to severe symptoms, medications — many of which are safe in breastfeeding — can help you recover faster and more completely.

Create boundaries unapologetically. It's okay to say no to visitors. It's okay to ask others to step in. It's okay to prioritise your peace over politeness.

Use the task priority model to protect your energy:

Do the Important & Urgent (e.g., baby care, your health)

Schedule the Important but Not Urgent (e.g., doctor appointments)

Delegate the Urgent but Not Important (e.g., errands)

Ignore the Not Important & Not Urgent (e.g., social obligations)

Make space for yourself. Even ten minutes of solitude — whether it's journaling, deep breathing, walking, or just sitting in silence — can help ground you and recharge your mind.

You don't have to do it all. You only need to do what's essential. The rest can wait. Your worth is not measured by productivity or perfection.

***"There is no way to be a perfect mother, but a million ways to be a good one."***

**— Jill Churchill**

And sometimes, being a good mother starts with being kind to yourself.

If you're reading this and nodding along, feeling seen — hold onto that. Healing begins with awareness, and strength grows from self-compassion. You are braver than you believe, more resilient than you know, and more loved than you feel right now.

You're not just nurturing a new life — you’re also re-learning how to love and care for yourself.

Let that be enough.✿

## Chapter - 4

# The Milk Dilemma - Breastfeeding, Lactation Struggles & Formula Feeding

They say breastfeeding is natural. That it will come easily. That the baby will just know what to do.

But the truth?

While breastfeeding is biological, it's also a skill — one that you and your baby learn together. And like any skill, it takes time, patience, and sometimes, a whole lot of support.

Let me start with my own story. I'm a doctor. I had attended lactation workshops, taught others about the benefits of breastfeeding, and could rattle off latch techniques in my sleep. I thought I was prepared.

Then my daughter was born.

And I froze.

She latched beautifully, but milk never came. I was exhausted. Every feed felt like a battle. I cried more than she did. And every time someone said, "Breastfeeding is the most beautiful bond," I wanted to scream, "It may be, if the milk ever came".

Because yes — it can be beautiful. But it can also be painful, frustrating, and filled with self-doubt.

❢ Take-home message:

*Breastfeeding is learned, not automatic. Be kind to yourself during this learning curve.*

## The physiology of Lactation

Lactation is a beautifully orchestrated physiological process, driven by a delicate hormonal dance that begins even before birth. Two key hormones — prolactin and oxytocin—are the stars of this show. Prolactin, secreted by the pituitary gland, is primarily responsible for milk production. Every time your baby suckles, it sends a signal to your brain to release more prolactin, telling your body, "Hey, we need more milk!" Oxytocin, on the other hand, governs the let-down reflex — it helps the milk already made to be released from the breast. It's triggered not just by suckling, but sometimes even by hearing your baby cry or thinking about your baby. This reflex causes the tiny muscles around the milk-producing glands to contract and push milk through the ducts towards the nipple.

Lactation works on a simple but powerful principle: supply meets demand. The more frequently and effectively your baby nurses (or milk is expressed), the more milk your body will be signalled to produce. That's why regular breastfeeding or pumping is key, especially in the early weeks, to establish a strong and steady milk supply. It's a relationship built on rhythm, touch, and trust — your body responding to your baby's needs in real time.

### *The Latch: Where It All Begins*

The first hurdle is often the latch. A good latch means the baby's mouth covers the areola, not just the nipple. The chin should touch your breast, the nose should be free, and you should hear soft swallowing — not clicking or smacking sounds. You can keep in mind the mnemonic CALM for checking for the latch when you start feeding.

C- Chin should be on the mother's breast

A- Areola in the mouth

L- Lower lip opened outward

M- Mouth Wide opened.

If feeding hurts beyond the initial seconds, if your nipples are cracked or bleeding, or if the baby seems unsatisfied after feeds, it's time to ask for help.

I once consulted for Shalini, a first-time mom, who dreaded feeding time. Her baby wasn't gaining weight, and she winced every time he latched. We called in a lactation consultant, tried different positions, used nipple shields for a while — and within a week, everything changed. Her baby began thriving. More importantly, Shalini stopped feeling like a failure.

**Take-home message:**

*Seek help early if breastfeeding hurts or isn't going well. Lactation consultants are lifesavers.*

## The Milk Supply Panic

Almost every new mom, at some point, whispers this fear: "Am I making enough milk?"

### Signs Your Feeds May Not Be Enough

It's natural to worry, but certain signs indicate that your baby may not be getting enough milk. These include fewer than 6 wet diapers a day after the first week, consistently poor weight gain, prolonged feeding sessions without satisfaction, or lethargy during feeds. If your baby seems unsatisfied even after long nursing sessions, or you're constantly anxious about their intake, it's worth checking in with your paediatrician or a lactation consultant.

### False Alarms: When it's Not Low Supply

Sometimes what looks like low milk supply is just a misunderstanding of normal behaviour. Cluster feeding— where your baby nurses frequently for a few hours — is not a sign of insufficient milk but a natural way to boost your supply. Soft breasts after the first few weeks, short feeds in older babies, or babies wanting to suck for comfort can also cause concern, but are often completely normal.

**Take-home message:**

*Milk production is supply and demand. Feed more, express more, and stay relaxed. Look for signs from your baby — not just the clock or the bottle.*

## Why Is My Milk Less?

There are several reasons why milk supply might dip, and most of them are beyond your control. A delay in initiating breastfeeding after birth, especially after a C-section or when the baby is in NICU, can impact the supply. Hormonal imbalances like thyroid issues or PCOS, excessive blood loss during delivery, inadequate calorie or fluid intake, stress, anxiety, and even certain medications or contraceptives can play a role.

Sometimes, it's simply about the baby's latch not being effective or the feeding sessions being too short or infrequent. And of course, the biggest culprit — self-doubt. The moment we start second-guessing ourselves, our bodies often follow suit, and the milk production comes down.

### *The Power of Breast Massage*

Breast massage can be a helpful tool to both stimulate milk production and ensure better drainage of milk during feeds or pumping. Gentle circular motions from the outer part of the breast towards the nipple before and during feeds can help open up blocked ducts and increase milk flow. It can also relieve engorgement and improve let-down reflexes.

You can use warm compresses before massaging and combine hand expression with pumping for better output. Doing this regularly can make a noticeable difference in comfort and supply, especially during the early weeks when the breasts are still adjusting to your baby's needs.

❢ Take-home message:

*Breast massage is a simple, effective way to support your milk flow and avoid common breastfeeding discomforts*

### *Hand Expression*

After my delivery I was told to pump milk and send to to NICU for Maanvi. All equipped with electric pump I started of, but to my surprise, nothing came. An aunt who is a Paediatrician came to visit me. She told me that in the initial days electric pumping is not useful and you must express it manually. I started pinching and pulling my breast but still nothing. That night thanks to google and my aunt who showed me the correct way of holding and expressing that the milk supply started and that gave me such a relief and so much confidence. You need to hold from the areola, push back to the chest and then pull front from the nipple for expressing. Just like milking the cow.

Follow these steps:

CUP around your breast in a C shape, 3 fingers distance from the nipple.

PRESS back to the chest wall

PRESS towards the nipple (without moving your hand from your breast)

### Boosting Milk the Natural Way

The good news? Nature has a few gentle nudges for your milk supply. Frequent nursing or pumping (especially after feeds) sends the right signals to your body to produce more milk. Staying well-hydrated and nourished— with foods rich in healthy fats, iron, and protein — makes a difference. Natural galactagogues like fenugreek seeds, fennel, shatavari, cumin water, and moringa have shown promise in traditional practices. Warm compresses, skin-to-skin contact, and breast massage also help stimulate flow. Most importantly, a calm and supported mom is more likely to produce milk— so focus on your peace as much as your pumping.

💡 Take-home message:

*Milk production is supply and demand. Feed more, express more, and stay relaxed.*

### Breastfeeding Techniques and Storage Know-How

Here are some common and comfortable breastfeeding positions:

**Cradle hold:** Baby lies across your body — ideal for older infants.

**Cross-cradle hold:** More control, better for newborns.

**Football hold:** Baby tucked under your arm — great after C-section.

**Side-lying:** Ideal for night feeds and exhausted moms.

Always align the baby's body and bring the baby to the breast, not the other way around.

Try different positions to find what's comfortable for both of you.

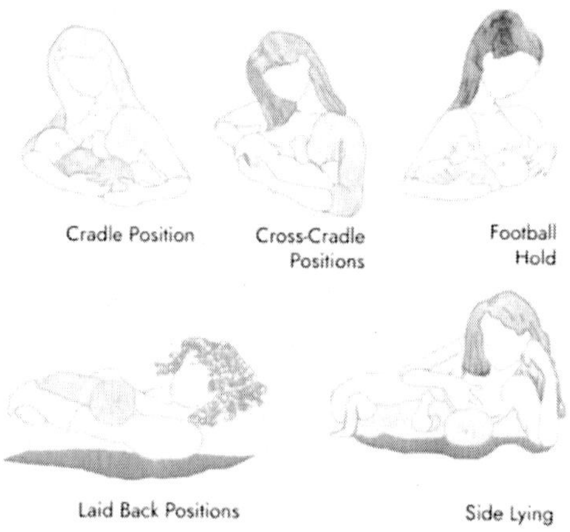

### Let's talk about breast milk storage for moms who pump:

**At room temperature (up to 25°C):** 3 hours

**In the fridge (4°C):** Up to 3days

**In the freezer:** 6 months (in a separate freezer), 3 months (if it's a compartment within the fridge)

Always store in clean bottles or breast milk storage bags. Label with date. When using frozen milk, thaw in warm water — not the microwave. And once warmed, use within 2 hours. Don't refreeze.

Breast milk can be safely expressed and stored, making feeding flexible. Expressed milk offers flexibility. Store it smart.

### *When should you introduce a bottle?*

Ideally, after breastfeeding is well established, usually after 4 weeks. Use a slow-flow nipple. Let someone else offer the bottle while you step away, so the baby doesn't get confused. And if the baby refuses the bottle, be patient. Try different temperatures, times of day, or positions.

### When Work Calls

Now, about returning to work. Many mothers worry about maintaining milk supply. It's possible. Pump every 3-4 hours during work hours. Invest in a good double electric pump. Carry ice packs and storage containers. Nurse before leaving and after returning. Some workplaces have lactation rooms now — ask HR.

Feeding routines may change, and that's okay. Some mothers switch to evening and night breastfeeding and formula during the day. Do what keeps you sane.

Working mothers can continue breastfeeding with planning and support.

Lastly, support is everything. Whether you breastfeed or you don't, whether you use formula from day one or later, what your baby needs most is you. The decision is yours, and you don't need to give any justification or explanation for your actions.

A loving, responsive, present mother is all your baby needs.

### *Formula Feeding – A Nourishing and Valid Choice*

Motherhood comes with so many decisions — and feeding your baby is one of the earliest and most emotionally loaded ones. While breastfeeding is often presented as the "gold standard," the truth is that formula feeding is a completely valid, safe, and nourishing alternative. Whether it's because of low milk supply, latching difficulties, maternal health concerns, or personal reasons, choosing to formula-feed is not a sign of failure — it's a sign that you are doing what's best for your baby and your family's overall well-being.

Many mothers struggle silently with guilt when they can't breastfeed exclusively, especially in cultures where breastfeeding is seen as the only "natural" way. But let's remember — what's natural is a mother making the best choice for her unique circumstances. Formula-fed babies grow up healthy, strong, and just as bonded with their parents. Feeding is about more than milk; it's about holding your baby close, responding to their needs, and sharing love in every cuddle-filled moment. Whether that nourishment comes from breast or bottle, what matters is that your baby is fed and you are mentally and physically well.

## The Basics of Safe Formula Feeding

If you're using formula, there are a few key practices that ensure your baby stays healthy and feeding is a stress-free experience. Hygiene is absolutely essential. Every bottle, nipple, cap, and accessory should be thoroughly washed and sterilised before each use, especially in the first year. You can do this by boiling them for 5–10 minutes, using an electric or microwave steam steriliser, or a UV steriliser if available. Make sure your hands are washed before preparing any feed.

When mixing formula, always follow the instructions on the box or tin. Use freshly boiled and cooled drinking water, never hot straight from the kettle, and never mix in more or less powder than recommended — this can either lead to inadequate nutrition or overload the baby's kidneys. The prepared formula should be used within one hour if left at room temperature. If you refrigerate it immediately after preparing, it can last up to 24 hours, but never reheat it more than once. And once the baby has started drinking from a bottle, discard any leftovers after an hour to prevent bacterial growth.

## Bottle Care and Practical Tips

Your feeding equipment needs regular attention. Replace bottles and nipples every 3–4 months, or sooner if they appear cracked, cloudy, or worn out. Choose bottles that are BPA-free and nipples that mimic the shape and flow of breastfeeding if you're combining both methods. Don't forget to inspect the flow of the nipple — newborns usually need slow-flow nipples, and you can move to faster flows as they grow. During feeds, hold your baby upright, close to your body, and never prop a bottle or leave them alone — it's unsafe and robs you both of those tender moments of bonding.

If your baby seems fussy during or after feeds, they may be swallowing air. Make sure to pause and burp them gently between and after feeding. Formula-fed babies may need fewer feeds than breastfed ones since formula digests a bit more slowly. But every baby is different, so follow your baby's cues. Some may want smaller, frequent feeds, while others may settle into a more spaced-out routine.

## A Bond That Goes Beyond the Breast

One of the biggest concerns mothers share is whether bottle feeding will impact their bond with their baby. The answer is no — bonding doesn't come from the source of nutrition, but from your presence, your voice, your gaze, and your love. Bottle feeding, when done mindfully, can be just as intimate as breastfeeding. Talk to your baby while feeding, stroke their skin, and make eye contact. You're building trust and attachment in these everyday moments.

And finally, don't forget to share the responsibility. Partners, grandparents, or siblings can also pitch in with bottle feeds, giving the mother some rest and helping everyone bond with the baby. This shared approach can ease the load and reduce exhaustion, which is so important in the early weeks and months.

Formula feeding is not second-best — it is simply another way to love and nourish your baby. With careful preparation, hygiene, and a loving touch, you can create a beautiful, calm, and safe feeding experience. What truly matters is that both baby and mother are healthy, happy, and thriving — however that journey looks.

### *Feeding Guilt: The unspoken battle*

Now let's talk about the most important part of breast feeding, the guilt associated with your supply or your choice of the way you want to feed your baby.

That painful internal battle between "I should breastfeed" and "I can't do this anymore."

Rina, a new mom, once called me sobbing. Her baby was screaming, her nipples were bleeding, and everyone around her just kept saying, "Try harder." She was spiralling. Eventually, she started supplementing with formula. That night, her baby slept. And so did she. The next morning, she smiled for the first time in weeks.

A fed baby is best. Breastfeeding is ideal, but formula is not a failure. Your mental health matters too.

### Let's bust a few myths while we're at it:

The formula is not poison. It's a scientifically developed alternative.

Formula-fed babies bond with their mothers, too.

Combination feeding (breast + formula) is absolutely fine.

Donor milk is a safe option in many cities through certified milk banks.

We don't talk enough about donor milk. In some cities in India, especially in larger hospitals, human milk banks now offer screened, pasteurised donor milk for babies in NICUs or those whose mothers can't produce milk initially. It's a safe and beautiful option if accessible. Also, remember to donate to these milk banks in case you are producing in excess rather than wasting it, as it can be of a lot of importance to another newborn.

There are many ways to feed a baby. Choose what works for you and your family.

I would like to share with you some stories of a few fellow mothers in detail that will help you connect with the message we wish to convey,and help you feel that you are not alone and that it's all okay.

## *Stories that you can relate to..*

### Sita and Geeta — Sisters, Milk, and Misunderstanding

Sita and Geeta were sisters who delivered their babies just weeks apart. Sita had a vaginal delivery, Geeta a C-section. Both babies were healthy. At their cradle ceremony, a well-meaning but thoughtless aunty started comparing deliveries and breastfeeding.

"C-section? Poor thing, you missed the real experience," she said to Geeta.

A seed of self-doubt was planted in Geeta that day. Her milk supply dwindled. Her baby had nipple confusion. Pumping became a desperate routine. Eventually, she was producing barely 30 ml a day. The guilt became unbearable.

Her husband and mother kept encouraging her, but it wasn't until he made her step outside — physically and emotionally — that healing began. Therapy, support groups, and self-care followed.

Ironically, a year later, it was Geeta's formula-fed child who was more active and emotionally connected, simply because Geeta had learned to be present, loving, and emotionally available.

💡 Take-home message:

*It's not about the source of milk. It's about the source of love.*

### Dr. Ira — the Paediatrician Who Struggled to Feed

Ira was a paediatrician — well-read, well-prepared, and passionately committed to exclusive breastfeeding.

But life had other plans.

A difficult delivery, a sleepy baby, poor latch, and low supply turned her dream into a nightmare. She pumped obsessively, refused formula, and slowly started disappearing into a fog of guilt and exhaustion.

When the paediatrician suggested formula, she broke down.

"You're not a milk machine," her husband reminded her. "You're her mother. She needs you whole."

That moment shifted everything. Slowly, with love and support, Ira found joy again — in her baby, in herself, and in her motherhood.

### 💡 Take-home message:

*In trying to do what's 'best,' don't forget what's good enough. And often, good enough is perfect.*

### Asha's Quiet Victory

Asha had a premature baby born at 32 weeks. She barely saw him in those first few days, as he stayed in the NICU on oxygen and IV fluids. She pumped diligently, desperately hoping her milk would nourish him.

But nothing came.

Each day, she stared at the pump, willing the milk to appear. Drops turned to ml, but it was slow and painful. Meanwhile, her baby was fed donor milk from the hospital's milk bank. Her relatives whispered that it was "someone else's milk" and questioned its safety.

She felt like a bystander in her own motherhood.

The NICU nurse took her aside and said, "You are still your baby's mother, even if you're not the one feeding him right now. He knows your voice. He feels your touch. Don't underestimate that."

Those words saved her.

When her baby finally came home, Asha had barely enough supply to feed him, but she held him skin-to-skin, talked to him, sang to him, and fed him formula when needed — without shame.

At six months, he was thriving on exclusive breast feeding. And so was she.

**💡 Take-home message:**

*Even when you can't give milk, you give love. That's what defines motherhood.*

### In Conclusion: Love Over Labels

Whether you breastfeed for two days or two years, whether your baby thrives on breast milk, formula, donor milk, or a combination — it doesn't define your worth.

The milk journey is rarely linear. It's full of learning curves, trial and error, and big emotions. But it's also full of love.

What matters is that you are present, loving, and responsive.

If you ever feel stuck, ask for help — from a lactation consultant, a paediatrician, or another mother who's been there. You don't have to figure it all out alone.

The feeding journey is rarely perfect. It's messy, emotional, and uniquely yours.

Feed with love. And give yourself some too.

### Take-home message:

*Feeding your baby is not just about nutrition. It's about connection, confidence, and compassion — for your baby, and for yourself.*

Breathe, mama. You're doing your best. And that's more than enough.

### Chapter - 5

# You're Not Alone - Building and Relying on Your Village – Role of Spouse, Parents, In – Laws, Siblings, Friends, Support groups.

In this chapter, I have explained in detail the role of the people around you – your support system. But sometimes, even well-meaning people may not understand how to help you. So the key here is communicating with them. If it's hard to talk to them, you may want to request that they just read the chapter ahead.

## *Role of the Husband*

The centre of your support system is your husband. So let us start from there.

In today's world, many husbands are becoming equal partners in parenting. But let's be honest — it's not just about changing diapers and attending parent-teacher meetings. This journey starts much earlier, ideally when you decide to marry each other. And the role of a husband becomes even more critical during the emotionally and physically challenging months of pregnancy and postpartum.

Marriage lays the foundation for what's to come. The deeper your connection and understanding now, the better you'll be able to support her when it matters most.

## Understanding Her World

A woman leaves behind her home, her parents, her comfort zone, and steps into a new world to build a life with you. She is not just looking for love; she is looking for belonging. She wants you to be the bridge that helps her integrate into your family, your routines, and most importantly, your life.

Husbands often underestimate how powerful the little things can be in marriage:

Give her undivided attention when she speaks.

Make time to enjoy each other away from family responsibilities.

Don't shy away from subtle public displays of affection—they remind her that she is cherished.

Include her in discussions, especially those you typically have with your parents alone.

When she raises concerns about your family, don't get defensive — listen. She's not attacking, she's asking for your support.

Be patient. She's learning to adjust.

Learn to pamper her during her period. Small gestures like keeping track of her cycle or bringing her favourite snack can mean the world.

And to the wives reading this, men aren't mind readers. If you need something — say it. Spell it out clearly. Most men are doers, problem-solvers. They need specifics. So instead of waiting for them to "just get it", tell them what you want, and teach them how to love you better.

## Before Pregnancy: Building a Safe Space

When planning for a child, it's not enough to talk about names or baby clothes. You must first listen to your partner's fears, doubts, and expectations. She might feel overwhelmed — after all, she's going to carry the baby, face physical exhaustion, and navigate emotional ups and downs. The decision must be mutual and supported with empathy.

What you can the husband do:

Stand by her when people ask about "when's the baby coming?"

Attend doctor appointments with her — not because she can't manage, but because your presence reassures her.

Don't hesitate to get tested for fertility issues if needed. It doesn't question your masculinity; it shows maturity.

If the pregnancy is planned, make it memorable.

If it was unplanned, reassure her that you're still thrilled and committed.

## During Pregnancy: Be Her Person

Pregnancy brings attention — congratulations, blessings, gifts. But often, people forget the woman behind the bump. She may feel like a vessel rather than a person. This is where you come in.

It's not just about bringing her water or lifting heavy bags. It's about emotional companionship.

Let me share a story that perfectly illustrates this.

Asha and Aryan had been married for 7 years and had finally conceived after years of trying. Rashmika and Rahul, on the other hand, had dated for 10 years and were married for just 6 months when they found out they were expecting. Despite the difference in journeys, both women were close friends and excited to be pregnant together. In their fifth month, the couple went on a holiday – the babymoon.

Aryan was dutiful — he gave Asha her medicines on time, carried her bags, and ensured she had everything she needed. But emotionally, he was distant — occupied with phone calls, TV, or beer with friends.

Rahul, in contrast, was present. He held Rashmika's hand, played card games, chatted with her, went on walks, and kept her engaged and reassured.

One evening, over dinner, Asha broke down. Despite being "taken care of", she felt alone. What she needed wasn't just help — it was connection.

This story reminds us, care is not just duty — it's presence.

Pregnancy triggers many questions in a woman's mind:

Will my husband still find me attractive?

Will I ever get my body back?

Will I be a good mother?

Will I be able to manage everything?

And if she senses you pulling away, even slightly, her mind can spiral into answering all those questions with a NO.

### So what should "he" do?

Compliment her often — on her looks, strength, and the journey.

Surprise her with little things — a note, a snack, a spa day.

Hold her hand in public. It says, "You belong. I'm here."

Be physically affectionate — even without sex. Intimacy can be emotional.

### Things You Can Do During Pregnancy

Be physically close — massages, cuddles, hand-holding.

Go for movies, drives, or walks — do things you both enjoy.

Give her medicines — this creates a sense of security.

If she can't lie down flat at night, be her pillow. Literally.

Be present for all major scans and check-ups.

If she says, "I need you today" — don't brush it off. She means it.

Prioritise her — yes, even before work, friends, or family.

Help her with daily chores.

Cook or get her favourite food. Cravings are real!

Plan a holiday or a small baby-moon if possible.

Help her prepare for delivery — shopping, classes, logistics.

Don't force family expectations — this baby is yours and hers.

Plan a baby shower or maternity shoot — make her feel celebrated.

**Most importantly:** Show up. Every. Single. Time.

## During Delivery: Don't Outsource Love

If permitted, be in the delivery room — whether it's a C-section or natural birth. Don't send her mom in while you wait outside comfortably. Your presence means everything.

Hold her hand, tell her she's strong, and remind her how much she means to you. When the baby is born, thank your wife before anything else. Hold the baby together.

These are sacred moments. Don't miss them.

## After Delivery: Be Her Anchor

Once the baby arrives, most of the attention shifts to the newborn. Relatives visit to see the baby. Everyone gushes over the little one. But very few check in on the mother.

She's sore, sleep-deprived, and emotionally fragile. And yet, she's expected to smile, feed, entertain visitors, and "bounce back." Amidst all the love for the baby, the mother often feels invisible.

Somewhere, she may even feel jealous — not because she doesn't love her baby, but because she misses the undivided attention she once received.

Here's what the husband can do:

When people come to meet the baby, make sure they acknowledge the mother, too.

Let her rest. Handle visitors. Don't expect her to play host.

Be patient. Her body and mind are healing.

Support her through breastfeeding challenges — don't give advice, give snacks, water, and hugs.

Encourage her if she wants to try pumping or formula — remind her there's no one perfect way.

Don't forget to just sit with her. Listen. Be there.

Remember: In the early days, she needs you more than ever. And your baby needs both parents — especially a mother who feels emotionally safe.

## Later in her postpartum journey

Postpartum is not just the first 40 days. It's not just about healing from stitches or a C-section. It's not just about the first lactation challenges or getting the baby to latch. Postpartum can last months, and for some women, it lingers in subtle ways for years — in her mind, her body, and her confidence.

The only way a woman survives it all? With ongoing support — not just from her husband, but from her entire circle.

The partner can be the mother's anchor in ways like – backing her for her decisions, small or big, giving her priority over your family and friends, making her feel that the love for her has only increased and that she is not a side character in her own film . The partner must always make the new mom feel wanted, respected and happy.

Let me tell you a story.

Neha's Fourth Trimester

Neha had a normal delivery and was sent home after two days. Her vaginal stitches healed quickly, and on the outside, she looked just fine. Her husband, Ravi, resumed work after a week, and her mother-in-law was around to help with the baby. Everyone assumed she was doing okay.

But Neha would cry in the bathroom every morning. Not because she didn't love her child — but because she was exhausted, in pain, leaking milk at random times, and had no one asking, "Neha, how are YOU today?"

It took a full breakdown during a paediatrician's visit for her husband to realise that Neha wasn't fine — she was just functioning.

Ravi changed from that day. He started watching the baby for two hours every night so Neha could sleep in another room. He made her join a WhatsApp group of new moms in the area. And on Sundays, he'd take her out, even if it was just a 30-minute drive with a coffee and no baby.

What changed? Not her situation — but the support.

## What Postpartum Support Should Look Like?

Here's what most new moms need, beyond the medical part:

**Time to rest:** Not just in the first week, but in the first few months. Someone who says, "You sleep, I'll watch the baby."

**Nutrition:** Healthy, warm meals without the guilt of not cooking. A bowl of dal with ghee, a fruit cut for her, or just her favourite filter coffee, made the way she likes it.

**Companionship**: Someone to talk to, without judgment. To listen to her frustrations and laugh with her when she cries because the baby pooped right after a diaper change.

**Validation:** A voice saying, "You're doing great, I know it's tough, and I'm proud of you."

The support of the spouse must be a constant thing in the journey of motherhood, where she feels that no matter what and when, her husband will always be on her side.

💡 Take-home message:

*You don't become a supportive husband and father the day your child is born. You grow into it — starting from the day you promised to love and cherish your wife.*

*Build your foundation during courtship. Strengthen it through the highs and lows of pregnancy. And lean into it during postpartum.*

*Because a strong husband doesn't just raise a healthy child — he builds a resilient woman, a happy family, and a partnership that truly lasts.*

*Show up. Be kind. Listen more. And never stop telling her:*

*"You're not alone. I'm here. We're in this together. Your spouse can — and should — be your first line of emotional defence. But they cannot be your only ones."*

## Role of Immediate Family — Parents and In-Laws

Let's talk about the supportive family unit we have in the Indian Setting, but sometimes a lack of communication can lead to unintentional harm.

A mother's parents and siblings are her first line of emotional defence. But often, they either don't know what to do or get too involved in the wrong way. The parents and siblings would always want the best for their child and sibling, respectively, but unknowingly they tend to force certain ways of parenting which may not be acceptable to the new mom. There is no right or wrong; it is just a choice that needs to be acknowledged, if not followed.

### Storytime

Meera and Her Mom

Meera gave birth to twins. Her own mother came to stay with her for the first month. Initially, it was a blessing — homemade food, the comfort of her mother's presence, and that magical way in which moms know how to swaddle a baby in 2 seconds flat.

But soon, the dynamics changed. Meera's mom started commenting on her milk supply, comparing her to her cousin, who "had so much milk she used to donate it." She would take over the babies, saying, "You rest, I'll manage," but wouldn't let Meera make her own decisions about feeding or sleeping schedules.

Meera felt sidelined in her own journey of motherhood.

Eventually, she sat down with her mom and cried. She said, "Amma, I need you to be here as my mother, not the baby's mother." That conversation turned things around. Her mother stepped back, helped with her instead of over her, and her siblings took over night shifts once a week so both mother and daughter could sleep.

### In-laws: Wisdom and Wounds

In India, the postpartum period often includes 40 days of rest at the maternal home, filled with traditional recipes, massages, and round-the-clock help. This can be a blessing. But sometimes, it also brings friction.

Rupa moved to her in-laws' house post-delivery. Her mother-in-law insisted that the baby be massaged with mustard oil and bathed daily, even when the baby had dry skin and a rash. "I felt helpless," Rupa said. "When I protested, I was told I was too 'modern' to understand."

We worked through it. I encouraged her to ask her husband to mediate. He spoke to his mother respectfully, bringing in the paediatrician's opinion. Slowly, they found a middle path.

Respect older generations but trust your instincts. Use your doctor's advice as a neutral ground. Frame disagreements as concerns for the baby's health—not challenges to tradition.

### The Middle Path: Navigating Generational Differences

Try saying, "Amma, I value your experience. Can we try this method for a few days and see how the baby responds?" or "The doctor suggested we do it this way—can I show you what she said?"

Compromise where it's safe. Hold your ground where it's not. And remember, parenting has evolved. What worked in 1980 may not work today, and that's okay.

### 💡 Take-home message:

*Choose your battles. Prioritise safety and sanity. Use love and logic — not confrontation — to bridge generational gaps.*

How Immediate Family Can Truly Help

Let her parent her way: Don't impose traditional practices unless asked. Share, but don't insist.

Be available without taking over: Ask before stepping in. "Do you want help with the feeding now?" is better than simply taking the baby away.

Respect her choices: Whether she breastfeeds, pumps, uses formula, or chooses a specific sleeping routine, back her up.

Support the husband, too: Encourage your son-in-law or brother-in-law to be involved. Don't assume it's "the woman's job."

## The Guilt of asking for help

In today's world, so many mothers feel an unexpected pang of guilt when asking their own parents or in-laws for help. Somewhere between trying to be the "perfect mother" and absorbing modern ideas of independence and self-sufficiency, we've forgotten that parenting was never meant to be a solo job. Our mothers did it with help. Their mothers did too. Yet today, we hesitate to ask for even a few hours of rest, or a warm meal, or a hand to rock the baby while we shower. "They've done their bit, why should I bother them now?" is something I hear often. But motherhood is not a performance, and strength doesn't mean doing everything alone. The guilt comes from internalised pressure to "handle it all," but the truth is: accepting help isn't a weakness — it's wisdom. When we involve our elders, we honour their role, their experience, and we allow our child to grow within a cocoon of generational love. Let go of the notion that asking for help is imposing. It's how the village was always meant to work. Instead of guilt, let there be gratitude. And if the fear is of judgment or unsolicited advice, set boundaries with kindness. Say, "I'd love your help with meals or baby care — it would mean the world." It's okay to need your people. You're not supposed to mother alone.

### Siblings are Under-rated

A shout out to the sisters and brothers who quietly fill in the gaps. Your WhatsApp messages checking in, your surprise food deliveries, your jokes that make her laugh on days she hasn't smiled — they mean more than you know.

One mom shared how her younger brother ordered her postpartum pads and nipple creams on Amazon and got them delivered with a note that said, "Not glamorous, but necessary." She said, "That's the most loved I've felt." Another story of another mother and her brother, Maya, a first-time mom in Mumbai, told me her younger brother was her postpartum saviour. "He made dal-chawal, walked the dog, and rocked the baby so I could nap. He became the 'fun mama' but also my anchor."

## Role of Friends and Relatives

Now let's talk about the outer circle — friends, cousins, neighbours, and those Facebook "aunties" who remember you only during baby showers and birthdays.

### The Right Kind of Friends

Let me introduce you to Priya and her friend circle of four — all of whom had babies within a span of one year. They made a pact. Every week, one friend would send lunch to another. No fancy meals. Just dal, sabzi, roti — and sometimes a chocolate bar on the side.

Every fortnight, they'd meet in someone's home with the babies. No makeup, no pretence — just messy buns, milk-stained T-shirts, and full hearts.

That support system kept Priya from spiralling into loneliness, especially because her in-laws were in another city and her husband travelled frequently.

Friendships in postpartum are lifesavers. Even the friend who sends a meme or asks, "Did you poop today?" (yes, that's a thing post C-section) can become your anchor.

### The Relatives Who Mean Well But...

Now, the tricky part — relatives. Everyone wants to visit the baby. But many come with opinions, judgments, and expectations.

"You've lost weight too fast."

"You've not lost weight yet?"

"You're not giving cow's milk?"

"You're holding the baby too much."

"You're not holding the baby enough."

Sound familiar?

One mom said, "My aunt came home and asked me why I was wearing pyjamas instead of a saree — 10 days after my delivery." Another said her cousin kept suggesting "nuskas" (home remedies) every day until she finally had to block her on WhatsApp for mental peace.

Relatives must understand: postpartum is not a time to critique — it's a time to serve, support, and shut up if needed.

How Friends and Relatives Can Help

Don't show up uninvited. Ask if it's a good time to visit. Respect "no visitors" rules.

Don't expect to be served. If you're visiting a new mom, carry food. Don't ask for chai.

Offer practical help. "Can I hold the baby while you eat?" "Want me to do the dishes while we talk?" — These mean the world.

Speak gently. No comparisons, no body-shaming, no baby advice unless asked.

Celebrate her, too. Everyone brings gifts for the baby. Bring something for her — even if it's just a hand cream or a bar of chocolate.

## *Support Groups: Real Talk, Real Relief*

Sometimes, your family doesn't understand what you're going through. That's when support groups become invaluable. Online platforms like Facebook mom groups, BabyCenter India, or local postpartum meet-ups are filled with moms navigating the same maze.

I remember one mom who was battling PPD and felt unheard at home. She joined an online postpartum support circle. "I cried on Zoom, and no one told me to stop. I wasn't crazy. I was just not alone."

Community is powerful. Seek your tribe — online or offline. Vulnerability becomes strength when it's shared.

Let me end with this: The African proverb says, "It takes a village to raise a child." But it also takes a village to raise a mother.

Create your own Village. It may not look like your mother's did. Maybe your parents live abroad. Maybe you have a full-time job and no extended family nearby. That's okay. Your village is who you choose to let in — your spouse, your best friend, your neighbour, your therapist, your nanny, your lactation consultant. To prepare for the village you could try answering the questions below.

Write down this list:

Who will help me with household chores?

Who can take care of the baby while I nap?

Who will listen when I need to vent?

Who can come over in an emergency?

Who will celebrate my baby's milestones with me?

Your village is built, not inherited. It takes effort — but it is worth every bit.

So build yours. Nourish it. Lean on it. Let go of guilt. And remember, asking for help is not a weakness — it's a strategy for survival. You are not alone. And you were never meant to be.

### Take-home message:

*Motherhood is beautiful, but it is also brutal in the beginning. It is raw, overwhelming, isolating, and riddled with doubt.*

*But it becomes bearable — even joyful — when she knows she's not doing it alone.*

*So whether you're the partner, parent, sibling, friend, or neighbour — show up. Not just for the baby, but for the mother who just became one.*

*And to all the new moms reading this — don't hesitate to ask. You are not a burden. You are a warrior in recovery.*

*And you deserve a village.*

*Chapter - 6*

# Stay-at-Home Mom or Working Mom: Both Deserve Respect and Choice

"I am a stay-at-home mom. I left my career behind because I wanted to be present for my child every moment of the day."

"I am a working mom. I work because I love my job, and it brings me joy and a sense of independence."

Aren't both these statements equally valid?

There's absolutely nothing wrong with either of them.

In today's fast-paced, constantly demanding world, many women work incredibly hard to carve out a place for themselves. After years of education, training, and experience, their careers are more than just jobs — they're a part of their identity and passion. So, when a woman gets pregnant, one of her biggest worries is whether she can continue doing what she loves or if motherhood will steer her in a different direction. Can she balance both? Will society give her that option?

In the Indian context, the burden of caregiving still largely falls on women. From generations past, the narrative has been that a woman's primary responsibility is toward her home, her family, and especially her children. So deeply ingrained is this belief that fathers are rarely conditioned to even think about how a baby might affect their careers. It's simply assumed that the woman will adjust, compromise, and carry the emotional and physical workload.

Now, this isn't to say that women should all be working and men should take over the homes. It's not a war between genders. But at the very least, we must push for the most basic right for mothers: the freedom to choose, without guilt. Whether a new mother decides to stay at home or return to work, it should be her decision. She shouldn't be made to feel ashamed if she's not contributing financially, nor should she be made to feel selfish if she chooses to continue her career.

Let's face it — today's women have gotten used to being financially independent, making decisions for themselves, and working toward their personal growth. Denying that suddenly after childbirth is not only unfair, but also mentally exhausting. A mother's happiness is foundational to her child's well-being. A content, supported, and fulfilled mother — whether she finds that fulfilment in raising her child at home or excelling at her workplace — can raise healthy, happy children.

And for anyone who looks down upon stay-at-home moms, let me just say this: raising a child is a full-time job. It's physically draining, mentally demanding, and emotionally overwhelming. As a doctor, I've often felt that being at the hospital is less exhausting than being at home all day. And yet, this immense effort often goes unacknowledged, leading to one of the biggest silent epidemics of our times — postpartum depression.

Our mothers may have stayed home, too, but the world they lived in was different. They don't always understand why we crave appreciation or why being at home makes us feel emotionally low. The answer lies in our evolving expectations. We were raised in a time when education and careers were emphasised. We were rewarded with paychecks, bonuses, and recognition at work. Our minds got used to being validated. So, when that validation disappears after we choose to stay home, the lack of appreciation feels like a void.

The bottom line? Whether or not to work after having a baby is a deeply personal decision. Every mother deserves the space and support to make that decision for herself.

Now I would like to share some stories with fictional names to make you feel and understand what I mean to convey in this chapter, and some aspects of the guilt trip.

### *Story Time*

#### Two Mothers, Two Journeys

Priya and Supriya had been best friends since their medical college days — two dedicated doctors who had walked side by side through exams, internships, and the rollercoaster ride of medicine. Priya had her baby girl in 2015 while she was still doing her post-graduation. It was a whirlwind phase. She took just three months of maternity leave before heading back to college, knowing she had to finish what she started. Her baby stayed at home, lovingly cared for by her mother and mother-in-law during the day. Every evening, Priya would rush home, scoop her baby into her arms, and give her every moment of undivided attention until the next morning.

After completing her degree, Priya decided to pause. She hadn't had enough time with her daughter in the early months, and it tugged at her heart. So she took a break—no job applications, no work commitments — just time at home, soaking in the precious everyday moments of motherhood. A year later, she eased back into work as a professor at a medical college. Even now, she gives her all at work during the day, and once she's home, she's fully present with her child.

Supriya's journey looked different. She got married after completing her post-grad and was already working at a reputed mid-sized corporate hospital. Known and loved by her patients and colleagues alike, she was thriving in her career. A year into marriage, she gave birth to her baby and took a six-month maternity break. But unlike Priya, she began returning to work in short bursts, gradually increasing her hours. By the time her baby was eight months old, Supriya was back to full-time work. But once she was home? That baby never left her arms. Every cuddle, every moment, every smile — she held onto them like gold.

So who did it right?

The answer is simple: both of them did. Because there is no single right way.

Every mother makes choices based on her circumstances, emotions, and needs. Priya had to return early to complete her education — but later made time to reconnect and be fully present. Supriya, on the other hand, was silently struggling with postpartum depression. Her therapist suggested she engage in something that brought her joy outside motherhood — and for her, that was her work. It helped her heal and become the mother she wanted to be.

We often hear people say, “The baby needs the mother most in the early days.” But let me ask you — when does a child stop needing their mother? I’m 33, a doctor, and a mother myself. And I still need mine. That’s the kind of bond we’re talking about.

Motherhood isn't about clocking hours. It’s not a requirement — it’s a relationship. A presence. A connection. Any time you spend with your child — whether it is 20 minutes or 20 hours — is sacred. It is not about the quantity; it’s the presence, the love, the intention.

### Take-home message:

*There’s no “right time” to be with your child. Every moment you get in your fullest present state is the right time. Because that bond isn’t built on a timetable — it’s built on love.*

## Presence over Perfection

Let's revisit our two sisters — Sita and Geeta. Both were talented, ambitious, and had built solid careers for themselves. Sita ran her own software company, while Geeta thrived in the creative world of interior design. From the moment they finished their education, both sisters had been on a mission — working hard, staying focused, and building a life of purpose and progress.

Their professional lives looked equally impressive. Meetings, deadlines, and back-to-back projects — both were busy and brilliant in their fields.

So what are we comparing here?

Well, it's not about ambition or success. It's about a small, often overlooked difference — one that had a quiet, yet powerful impact on their children.

You see, Geeta, despite managing multiple interior design projects and having a full calendar, followed one simple rule: once she was done with work for the day, she truly unplugged. Her evenings were sacred. The moment she got home, the phone was put away, the laptop shut, and the rest of the day was all about her child. They danced in the living room, splashed in the bath, sang silly songs, played with blocks, and giggled till bedtime. She wasn't perfect, and the stress was real— but she had made a choice. After work, her child got the best of her — not the leftovers.

Sita, on the other hand, was unknowingly slipping into a pattern many of us can relate to. The lines between work and home blurred. Emails followed her home, meetings bled into dinner time, and even while sitting beside her kids, her mind was busy elsewhere. On holidays, she'd often catch up with friends or keep scrolling through her phone while the kids played nearby. She loved her children deeply — but she wasn't fully present.

And that made a difference.

It's not about working less. It's about being more present when you're home with your children. Children don't need fancy toys or hour-long activities — they just need you. Your full attention. Your engaged presence. Your genuine laughter. Your arms wrapped around them without a phone in one hand.

### Take-home message:

*It's absolutely okay to be a working mother — your ambition is not something to feel guilty about. But just like you give 100% to your job, your children also deserve a version of you that isn't distracted. Create clear boundaries. Guard your post-work hours like they're sacred. Because to a child, your undivided presence feels like love — and that's what they remember.*

### Anecdote:

I remember one evening when I came home after a long day at the clinic, still mentally sorting through lab results and pending reports. My toddler came running to me with a picture she had drawn. I nodded absentmindedly, barely looking. She quietly folded the paper and walked away. That moment stayed with me. I had missed *the moment*. Since then, I made myself a promise: when I'm with her, I'm truly *with her*. Everything else can wait. I changed some things in my practice. I stopped attending to every phone call that came buzzing and distracting me from my Maanvi time. I informed and habituated all my patients and the hospital alike that I am available only on WhatsApp messaging after office hours, and I will get back to them at my convenience or rather, when my daughter is busy with something else.

## The Stay-at-Home Myth

Let's take another pair of women — Sneha and Shreya. Both are stay-at-home moms. Both come from supportive, well-to-do families. Working outside the home wasn't a compulsion for either — it was a choice, and they had chosen to stay home to raise their children.

But staying at home means different things to different people. Let me show you a regular day in each of their lives.

Sneha wakes up by 7 a.m., starts her day with some light exercise or meditation, and uses that quiet morning hour to ground herself before the day begins. At 8 a.m., she gently wakes her little one and gets her ready — with help from the household staff, yes — but Sneha is actively involved in every bit. She chats, sings, plays, bathes, and feeds. Her child's morning routine is filled with attention and care.

By 9 a.m., her toddler is fed and content, playing independently while Sneha gets ready and finishes some chores. At 11, after a quick cuddle and a warm glass of milk, the baby naps. Sneha uses this time to run errands or catch up with a friend — but always returns before the child wakes. Afternoons are spent together — reading books, playing peek-a-boo, laughing under the fan on lazy floor mats.

Evenings follow a similar rhythm: snacks, outdoor time, bath, dinner, and bedtime. After the child sleeps, Sneha carves out time for herself and her husband. It's not a picture-perfect day — but it's structured, intentional, and connected.

Now let's talk about Shreya.

She wakes up only when her baby does — usually with the sound of crying at 8 a.m. She hands the baby to the helper while she freshens up and scrolls through social media over breakfast. The nanny bathes and dresses the baby. Shreya watches reels while her child plays. The day moves along in fragments — feeding, napping, some tantrums. And when the baby cries or gets too cranky, the screen comes out again. YouTube or cartoons to calm the child. Shreya, meanwhile, catches up on rest or gets ready to go meet friends in the evening.

By the time she returns home, the house is chaotic, the child overstimulated, and dinner still not ready. Her husband walks into a tired, distracted home. Shreya complains of exhaustion, lack of time for herself, and how hard it is to manage everything — even though she's been home all day.

But here's the truth: being at home doesn't automatically mean you're present.

Sneha and Shreya both made the same choice — to be stay-at-home mothers with house help for thei comfort. But their mindset, their intentionality, and their involvement were worlds apart.

### Take-home message:

*Staying at home can be beautiful and fulfilling — but only if done with awareness. Just like office work, it needs structure, routine, and purpose. You don't need to do everything yourself, but the time you do spend with your child should be real, mindful time. Bathing, dressing, feeding, cuddling, storytelling — these aren't chores; they're the threads that weave a strong mother-child bond.*

*You can make time for yourself. But you must also make use of your time with your child. Because that is the time they and, more importantly, you will remember and cherish when they grow up.*

### Anecdote:

When I took a break from work to stay home with my daughter, I wasn't sure what to expect. I had always been a working woman, constantly on the move, seeing patients, on the rounds, juggling hospital work and Clinic. But those days at home with her — doing simple things like brushing her tiny teeth together, picking picking out her clothes, making silly faces during bath time, or singing made-up songs while feeding her without any worry to rush for work — brought me a kind of joy that is hard to explain.

I remember one afternoon, we were sitting by the window, watching the rain. She pointed at every little thing — "car!", "dog!" - and I'd repeat them back with the same excitement. We were just… there. Together. Fully present. No screen, no rush, no distractions. Just us. That day, I realised I wasn't missing out on anything by being away from work. In fact, I was gaining something far more precious — the gift of uninterrupted connection.

Those moments weren't always glamorous or easy, but they were *real*. And they filled my heart in a way no professional achievement ever had.

*Quote:*

"Being with your child isn't about where you are. It's about who you are when you're with them."

Coming to the end of the chapter, I am now going to give you some workable solutions to maximise time with your children and also help you in time management for yourself and your chores, whether you are working or a stay-at-home mom.

### *Tips and Tricks for Working Moms to Maximise Time with Their Child*

Use your commute time for mental planning so you can be fully present when home.

Set clear boundaries — work hours end at a specific time.

Involve your child in simple household chores — it turns into bonding time.

Do one dedicated daily activity — reading a bedtime story, brushing teeth together, or having a short morning cuddle session.

Batch household tasks on weekends to free up weekday evenings for family.

### *Cheat Sheet Schedule for Working Moms*

#### Morning:

6:00 am – Wake up, self-care, exercise and plan the day

7:00 am – Breakfast with child, dress-up bonding time

8:00 am – Hand off child to caregiver/school, commute

#### Evening:

6:00 pm – Home from work, no screens, child-only time, dinner prep with child play

7:30 pm – Dinner together as a family

8:30 pm – Bath/story time with child

9:00 pm – Sleep routine for child

9:30 pm – Wind-down and me-time

### *Caregiver's Exhaustion for Stay-at-Home Moms*

Stay-at-home moms often work around the clock without recognition. Unlike a job where breaks are defined, and appreciation comes in performance reviews or salary hikes, this role is 24x7 with little validation. The result? Burnout. The endless loop of cooking, cleaning, feeding, bathing, teaching, and disciplining can drain anyone — especially when there's no break or adult interaction.

### How to Overcome Loneliness as a Stay-at-Home Mom?

Schedule regular meetups or calls with friends or other moms.

Enrol in a short online class or hobby group — something just for yourself.

Step out for a walk daily — even 30 minutes outdoors can uplift your mood.

Create small rituals — like a solo tea time or journaling— to feel grounded.

### *Cheat Sheet Schedule for Stay-at-Home Moms*

#### Morning:

7:00 am – Wake up, exercise or quiet time

8:00 am – Child's wake-up, bath, and breakfast routine

10:00 am – Play/learning activities with the child

#### Afternoon:

12:00 pm – Lunch and child's nap time (your me-time)

2:00 pm – Household chores or outings

#### Evening:

4:00 pm – Snack and outdoor play

6:00 pm – Dinner prep, play while cooking

7:30 pm – Family dinner

8:30 pm – Child's sleep routine

9:00 pm – Relax, read, or spend time with spouse

Children, no matter their age, thrive on routine, structure and discipline. Here are some examples of routines which you could tweak according to your comfort while maintaining good eating and sleeping routines the same. The more structure and schedule you have in your life, the better control you will have over work, kids, family and chores. You will always feel that you are ahead of your checklist and still are able to make so much time for yourself and your family. Create one that suits you. Stick to it, but don't beat yourself up for wavering from it a little bit or occasionally.

### Final Thoughts:

Going to work or staying at home doesn't define your motherly instinct. It's a personal choice which does not need any explanation to anyone but yourself. Whatever decision you do make, remember you are a mother and no matter what and how, you have to give 200 % to the baby that's come into yourworld. To do the same, sometimes the career, though going on, can take a backseat, and homely duties can go to 5th gear, but always remember that your life has parallel things going on all at the same time. Sometimes something can require more time and attention, and thus the other things must take a backseat.

*Chapter - 7*

# Back to the Grind - Returning to Work without Losing Yourself

Returning to work after having a baby is one of the most emotionally and physically challenging transitions a mother can face. It's a moment of mixed emotions — excitement to re-engage with the professional world, yet a deep tug of guilt and uncertainty about leaving your baby behind. The question most new mothers face isn't "Should I go back?" but "How can I do this and still feel like myself?"

❢ Take-home message:

*Returning to work isn't about choosing between your career and your baby. It's about finding a way to thrive in both.*

I vividly recall a conversation I had with my patient, Neha, who had been on maternity leave for six months. She was a lawyer, passionate about her work, but the thought of leaving her three-month-old daughter with a nanny was tearing her apart. "I love my job, but every time I think about leaving her, I feel like I'm betraying her," she said, her voice quivering. "How do I make this work?"

Your emotions are valid. Navigating motherhood and work can be a delicate balance, but it is possible with preparation and support.

### *Preparing to Return to Work*

Returning to work after having a baby is a deeply emotional and practical milestone. It's a mix of anxiety, excitement, guilt, and anticipation — sometimes all in one day. Many new mothers, especially in the Indian context, grapple with societal expectations, internal guilt, and the sheer logistics of managing a household and career. But with thoughtful preparation, this transition can be made smoother and less emotionally taxing.

The first and most essential step is mental preparation. It's natural to feel guilty about leaving your baby at home or in someone else's care, but remember — choosing to return to work does not mean you're any less of a mother. It's important to affirm your identity beyond motherhood, and for many, a professional role contributes to that sense of self. Start by visualising how your day will look, how you'll manage drop-offs, feeding schedules, your work hours, and your mental bandwidth. If possible, begin part-time or with reduced hours to ease the transition.

Next, consider the practical arrangements. Finding the right childcare support — whether it's a day care, a trusted nanny, or a family member — is central. Look for someone aligned with your parenting style. Spend time with them and your baby together before the actual return so that your baby can adjust and you can observe. Also, communicate clearly with your caregiver about feeding schedules, nap routines, comfort techniques, and emergency protocols

Also, prepare your baby for your absence gradually. Start by stepping away for short intervals during the day while someone else soothes or feeds the baby. This builds the baby's confidence in other caregivers and reduces separation anxiety for both of you. Leave them with familiar objects like your dupatta, a favourite toy, or a blanket that smells like you.

Don't forget self-care. You're going to be juggling a lot— physical recovery, emotional adjustment, disrupted sleep, and now, work. Prioritise rest when possible, eat nourishing meals, and talk to your partner about how household duties and parenting can be shared. Revisit expectations — maybe the house won't be perfect, but your peace matters more.

Talk to your employer or HR about flexible working hours, hybrid options, or backup leave policies. Having clarity on your work boundaries helps you feel more in control and reduces work-related stress. Set realistic goals initially; you don't have to overperform to "prove" yourself.

Finally, be kind to yourself. Every mother's return-to-work journey looks different. You may cry on the first day, check your phone a hundred times, or feel distracted. That's okay. With time, it gets better. You're doing this not just for your professional growth, but also to show your child that motherhood and ambition can coexist beautifully.

Neha, who had a demanding legal career, took several steps to prepare. She started preparing her daughter for time away by practising short separations, leaving her with a trusted family member while she ran errands. This helped ease both Neha's and her baby's transition when it was time for her to go back to work.

❢ Take-home message:

*Preparation is key to reducing anxiety. Start small with separations, and plan your childcare early.*

### Managing Pumping Schedules

If you're breastfeeding, one of the biggest hurdles in returning to work is figuring out how to continue providing breast milk for your baby. The good news is that with a little planning, you can make it work. It's essential to set a routine that works both for you and your baby, especially when it comes to pumping.

Start by investing in a good-quality breast pump. There are many options available today, from manual to electric pumps, and some are designed to be discreet and portable. Practice using the pump at home well before your first day back at work. This helps you get comfortable with the process and establishes a rhythm.

I remember another patient, Ritu, a software engineer who had to return to work after her 12-week maternity leave. She decided to exclusively pump. "It wasn't easy at first. I had to set reminders for pumping breaks at work, and sometimes it felt like the entire office was hearing the hum of my breast pump during meetings," she shared, laughing. "But I did it. And I'm glad I stuck with it."

Take-home message:

*Breastfeeding doesn't have to stop when you return to work. It's all about planning, persistence, and having the right tools.*

A good rule of thumb is to pump every 3-4 hours to keep up your milk supply, and try to pump at the same times each day. If you're pumping at work, make sure your office has a private space. Ideally, this space should be clean, comfortable, and free from interruptions. Keep your milk in a cooler bag with ice packs until you can store it in the fridge. Your employer is legally required to provide a private space for breastfeeding mothers, so don't hesitate to request one if needed.

## Handling Separation Anxiety

Separation anxiety is one of the most common emotions mothers experience when returning to work. You've spent months bonding with your baby, and the thought of leaving them in someone else's care can feel unbearable. But you're not alone. Most mothers experience this to some degree, and it's completely normal.

The key to easing separation anxiety is gradual separation and building trust with your childcare provider. Take small steps before your official return. A few weeks before starting back, start leaving your baby with the caregiver for a few hours at a time. This will help you both adjust to the idea of being apart.

Neha, for instance, took two weeks before returning to her full-time work schedule. During that time, she worked from home and gradually increased the hours she was away. This eased her nerves, and her daughter adjusted more easily to the separation.

**Take-home message:**

*Gradual separation helps both you and your baby adjust to the change. It's okay to feel anxious — just don't let it hold you back from taking that step.*

Your emotions are valid. Navigating motherhood and work can be a tough balance to keep, but it is possible with support, preparation and communication.

### Navigating Workplace Expectations

Once you've prepared at home, it's time to turn to your workplace. Whether you're returning to an office, working remotely, or on a flexible schedule, it's important to set clear expectations with your employer.

Start by discussing your work hours, deadlines, and how your pumping or childcare needs will be accommodated. Don't be afraid to ask for breaks for pumping or express your need for flexibility, especially in the first few weeks.

Another mother, Priya, a project manager, told me, "At first, I felt like I had to prove myself all over again. I didn't want to seem less committed because I had a baby. But I realised, I needed to be honest with my team.

Once I started having open conversations about my needs, things got easier."

💡 Take-home message:

*Set clear boundaries with your workplace. Be open about your needs and communicate them regularly.*

It's essential to build a support network at work, too. Seek out other mothers who can give advice or share tips on balancing work and parenting. Having colleagues who understand your challenges can make a huge difference in how supported you feel.

## Rebuilding Confidence at Work

Returning to work can be a confidence booster, but it can also feel like a setback, especially if you're dealing with self-doubt or body changes. It's natural to question your abilities after spending months focused on your baby. But remember, you are still the same capable, competent person you were before.

The first few weeks might be tough as you adjust to a new routine and schedule. But with time, you'll get back into your groove. Be kind to yourself. Permit yourself to feel uncertain or less than perfect. Your worth as an employee or a mother isn't tied to whether you're "doing it all" perfectly.

💡 Take-home message:

*Confidence comes with time and practice. Be patient with yourself.*

Ritu, the software engineer I mentioned earlier, had moments of doubt when she returned. "At first, I felt like I had to be on top of everything — work, breastfeeding, cooking, cleaning. But then I realised, it's okay to ask for help. It's okay to set boundaries. I'm still a good employee and a good mom, even if things aren't perfect."

❢ Take-home message:

*It's okay to ask for help. Confidence isn't about doing it all — it's about doing what works for you.*

### Final Thoughts

Returning to work doesn't mean you're leaving behind your role as a mother. It's an opportunity to rediscover yourself, build new routines, and show your child the power of balance. It's okay to feel nervous, guilty, or overwhelmed — it's all part of the journey. But remember, you're not alone. Countless mothers have walked this path, and you will find your rhythm, too.

The most important thing is to take it one step at a time. Celebrate small victories — like making it through your first day, or pumping enough milk for your baby. Lean on your partner, your colleagues, and your friends for support. Most importantly, trust yourself. You are doing something incredible, and you're doing it with love and grace.

❢ Take-home message:

*Returning to work is a transition. Take it slow, be kind to yourself, and know that you can succeed in both worlds.*

## *Careers – A Pause, Not the End*

Motherhood and career — two words that, when said together, can stir a storm of emotions. For many women, these aspects of life are deeply interwoven. And yet, when motherhood enters the picture, it often feels like we're being asked to choose between ambition and presence. But does it have to be a choice?

***"You can do anything — but not all at once."***

**— Oprah Winfrey**

Let me share a chapter from my own life, one that might resonate with you if you've ever felt torn between your career and your child.

Until the eighth month of my pregnancy, I was a practising physician — fully immersed in my work and loving it. My days were split between a reputable corporate hospital in the mornings and my clinic in the evenings. That small clinic was a dream I and my husband had slowly brought to life, brick by brick, patient by patient. After two years of effort, I had built a modest but growing practice. I was seeing 10–15 patients in just two hours— an encouraging number for someone early in her independent journey as a doctor.

Everything was moving steadily, and I was proud of how far I had come.

But as my due date approached, I moved to my mother's house for the delivery. Her home was far from both my own house and my clinic. I had no choice but to pause my evening practice. For the first time in years, I wasn't working — and I felt an ache I hadn't expected. Not just the discomfort of pregnancy or the upcoming delivery, but the weight of watching something I had worked so hard to build slowly drift out of reach.

***"Sometimes the strength of motherhood is greater than natural laws."***

**— Barbara Kingsolver**

After six months, I returned home and tried to restart my clinic — this time only by appointment. I thought it would be a smooth transition. But things didn't go as planned. Many days, I had no appointments at all. In fact, two or three days a week, the clinic would stay completely empty. It was disheartening. It felt like my career had hit a wall, and all the momentum I had built had simply disappeared.

I remember feeling dejected, sometimes even questioning myself. Had I made a mistake? Was stepping back from my work the wrong decision? Was I falling behind?

But then, something shifted. One quiet afternoon, I sat with my daughter as she tried to clap her hands for the first time. She looked at me with those curious little eyes and giggled when she succeeded. It was such a small thing. But in that moment, it felt like the most important thing in the world.

And I realised — I would never get this time again.

That phase — those first few months and years — is so fleeting. Babies don't stay babies. They grow quickly. And the absolute dependence they have on their mothers in the early stages is something that fades. Slowly, friends, school, and their world begin to take shape. And one day, you might find yourself asking them for time, waiting for a moment of connection that once came freely.

***"Children are not a distraction from more important work. They are the most important work."***

**— C.S. Lewis**

So I told myself something I hope every mother reading this will remember: It's okay to pause.

Your career can wait. Your child's early moments won't.

And when the time is right, you can rebuild. You can restart. You can even reinvent.

What we once created, we can create again. Maybe not in the same way, but often with more strength, depth, and meaning.

I like to think of life as a book — not a straight path, but a series of chapters.

There's a chapter for your education, one for your passion, one for your family, your health, your relationships, and of course, your career. These chapters don't close. They evolve. At different stages, you'll be more immersed in one chapter than another. And that's how it's supposed to be.

"Life is not about having it all. It's about having what matters most at the right time."

Right now, you may be in the "motherhood" chapter, and that might mean your "career" chapter has fewer pages at the moment. But that doesn't make it less important. It's simply waiting — waiting for you to return when you're ready, with a fuller heart and richer experience.

I'm reminded of a powerful metaphor I once came across — maybe you've seen it too. A professor shows his class an empty jar. First, he fills it with large rocks. Then he adds pebbles. Then sand. And finally, water. He asks the students if the jar is full at each stage, and each time, there's still space for something smaller.

He explains:

The big rocks represent the truly important things — health, family, meaningful work.

The pebbles are secondary priorities — social circles, achievements, material comforts.

The sand is the filler — social media, gossip, distractions.

And the water? It's the minor irritations and negativity—stress, comparison, judgment.

If you fill your life with sand and water first, you won't have room for the rocks. But if you place the big rocks first, everything else will find space around them.

***"The key is not to prioritise what's on your schedule, but to schedule your priorities."***

**— Stephen Covey**

This is how we must think about our lives. Your child, your health, your well-being — these are your big rocks. Your career, too, when the time is right, can be one of those big rocks. But only you get to decide the order.

For me, choosing to step back from my career wasn't easy. But I now see that it was necessary. It gave me the chance to bond with my daughter in a way I would never trade for anything — not even the most successful career.

And here's the truth: Motherhood doesn't erase your dreams.

It may delay them, reshape them, or even reroute them—but it never ends them.

You're not falling behind. You're just walking a different path, and that path is still leading somewhere beautiful.

So, if you're a mother struggling with a pause in your professional life, I want you to read this aloud: *I am not alone. I am not failing. I am living a chapter that matters deeply.*

Always believe that when the time comes to turn the page, your story will continue — with new purpose and renewed strength.

"You can be a good mom and still pursue your dreams. You're allowed to do both."

Careers can restart. Dreams can evolve. Passions can reignite.

But the moments with your child? Those only come once.

Choose what matters now — and trust that everything else will follow.

## Chapter - 8

# Rediscovering Intimacy - Love, Sex, and Partnership after Baby

When a baby enters your world, everything changes. Your body, your sleep, your priorities, your sense of identity — and yes, your relationship too. For many new mothers (and fathers), intimacy takes a backseat — not because love is lost, but because life has shifted in the most dramatic way.

### *Intimacy Is Not Just About Sex – Rebuilding Connection in a New World*

Let's get one thing straight right at the start: intimacy is not the same as sex. That's a misconception that puts unnecessary pressure on couples, especially new parents. In fact, in the early days after childbirth, physical intimacy in the form of sex is often the farthest thing from a mother's mind. And that's completely okay.

So, what does intimacy mean now?

Intimacy is a feeling of closeness, a sense of being seen, heard, and valued. It's the quiet tea made without asking. It's the foot rub at the end of a long day. It's the warm glance when the baby finally falls asleep. It's knowing someone has your back, even when your breasts are leaking, your stitches are sore, and you haven't showered in two days.

Neha, a first-time mother from Delhi, told me, "My husband and I didn't have sex for months. But every night, he would ask me, 'How are you feeling today?' and just sit with me. That kept us close." That's the kind of emotional intimacy that builds the foundation for everything else.

Ways to connect that aren't about sex:

Cuddle in bed without expectations.

Take a short walk together while the baby naps in a stroller.

Cook a meal together or eat in candlelight after the baby sleeps.

Listen to each other without giving solutions.

Send a sweet message during the day — just a simple "Thinking of you" can spark connection.

Practice skin-to-skin contact — not just for the baby, but between partners too.

## The importance of emotional, social, and spiritual intimacy

Many couples report feeling more deeply connected during the postpartum phase, even if they're not physically intimate. That's because surviving sleepless nights, decoding baby cries, and sharing responsibilities create a strong emotional bond. But only if both partners are present and participating.

Social intimacy might mean laughing over a silly Instagram reel or chatting about topics other than the baby. Spiritual intimacy could be as simple as holding hands in silence, praying together, or sharing what brings you peace in the middle of chaos.

One mom told me, "Every morning, my husband and I take 10 minutes to sit on the balcony and have chai before the day starts. That's our ritual. It's sacred." These small acts build closeness.

## The pressure to "bounce back" sexually

There's an unspoken narrative that things should return to "normal" quickly — that you should be ready for sex within weeks, that your body should look like your pre-pregnancy self, that desire should magically reappear.

The truth? For most women, it doesn't. And again, that's okay.

Postpartum is a time of healing, adjusting, and rediscovering. There's bleeding, hormonal shifts, vaginal soreness, stitches, body image changes, nipple pain, exhaustion — the list is endless. Expecting someone to be in the mood for sex in the midst of all this is unrealistic.

What matters more is acknowledging this reality together.

Give the mother time. Let her set the pace. Don't make jokes about how "long it's been." Don't pressure her to perform or reassure. Just be present. Be tender. Be patient.

❢ Take-home message:

*You don't "get back" to intimacy. You build it, piece by piece, in new ways that reflect the life you've created. Let go of timelines. Focus on connection. The rest will follow.*

### Understanding between Partners – Communication, Consent, and Coming Together

In the first part, we redefined intimacy; now let us learn to walk toward it again — together. Because if there's one truth that holds through the stormy nights and diaper explosions, it's this: no matter how deeply you love each other, you can't read each other's minds.

That's where communication comes in.

Postpartum life is noisy — with baby cries, doorbells, laundry machines, and that constant mental checklist of "things to do." But amidst all this noise, the most important conversations often get silenced.

Let me share a story.

Meera and Arjun, new parents in their early 30s, came to me during a follow-up visit. Meera was tearful, feeling disconnected from Arjun. "He just doesn't touch me anymore," she said. Arjun looked confused. "I thought you didn't want to be touched," he said softly. "You seemed tired all the time."

There it was — a classic example of love lost in translation. No anger. Just a gap in understanding. He was trying to respect her space. She was interpreting it as distance. Neither had actually asked the other what they needed.

Say it out loud. Even if it feels awkward.

Talk about your wants and don't-wants. Say, "I feel too sore for sex, but I'd love to cuddle tonight." Or "I miss feeling close to you — can we just hold hands while we talk?"

You're not the same couple you were before the baby. You're parents now. But you're also still lovers, friends, and you need to find new rhythms. And rhythm begins with real talk.

Things to say and ask each other:

> "What are you missing most about us?"
>
> "What can I do to help you feel more relaxed?"
>
> "Are you okay with this touch?"
>
> "Would you rather nap or go for a short walk together?"

> "I'm feeling nervous about getting intimate again — are you?"

Communication includes consent, every single time.

Postpartum bodies go through a massive transformation. Even if your partner has been cleared for intercourse medically, you still need enthusiastic consent. It should be a "yes" said with comfort and clarity — not a reluctant, guilt-ridden nod.

Sneha, a second-time mother from Pune, once told me, "The first time around, I felt pressured to resume sex quickly. I didn't want to disappoint my husband. But I wasn't ready. And that stayed with me, for years."

That's the thing — rushing into physical intimacy without emotional readiness can cause long-term damage. It chips away at trust. It creates an association between touch and discomfort. And eventually, it becomes a wall.

On the other hand, when partners take the time to listen, reassure, and accept each other's timelines, it builds safety.

Seeking help is a strength, not a failure.

If you've been trying to talk but keep ending up in arguments or silences, consider seeing a therapist or counsellor — either individually or as a couple. Many couples benefit from just a few sessions of guidance to learn how to express needs, manage expectations, and reconnect.

And if either of you is struggling with postpartum depression or anxiety, it's even more important to seek support. Mental health deeply affects intimacy, and sometimes what feels like relationship issues are actually symptoms of emotional exhaustion or hormonal imbalance.

Intimacy doesn't thrive in pressure. It blooms in patience.

Be kind to one another. Reassure each other. Laugh together when things get messy (and they will). If the baby spits up mid-cuddle, laugh. If you fall asleep halfway through a romantic moment, smile and try again another day.

### Quotes from real moms:

"My husband didn't understand how touch could feel irritating when I was breastfeeding all day. But once I explained it, he gave me space — and I felt so seen."

"We started scheduling 10-minute check-ins every night. It sounds silly, but it changed everything."

### 💡 Take-home message:

*Your partner is not your enemy. They are your teammate. Communicate with love, not assumptions. Ask, don't guess. Share, don't suppress. When in doubt, go back to basics: look into each other's eyes and say, "How are you really feeling?" That one question can change the entire mood of the room*

## *The Medical Side of Desire – Why it's Not Just in Your Head*

Let's talk about something many mothers whisper about in guilt:

"I just don't feel like having sex anymore. Is something wrong with me?"

The short answer? No, there's nothing "wrong" with you.

The long answer? Your body and mind have been through a monumental transformation, and sexual desire doesn't always bounce back right away. And that's okay.

"Why don't I feel like it anymore?"

This question has multiple answers, and most of them aren't your fault.

### 1. Hormonal Changes:

After delivery, your estrogen levels — especially if you're breastfeeding — can remain low for months. This affects vaginal lubrication, elasticity, and even natural arousal. You may experience dryness, irritation, or pain during intercourse.

Your body, in its infinite wisdom, is prioritising survival. It's producing high levels of prolactin (which supports milk production) and oxytocin (which helps you bond with your baby). But these same hormones can suppress libido.

Think of it this way—your body thinks, "Hey, we're nurturing a new baby. This is not the time for another pregnancy!" So it turns the dimmer down on your sexual appetite.

2. **Physical Recovery:**

Even if your delivery was smooth, your perineum (the area between the vagina and anus) may have undergone a lot — especially if there were stitches, a tear, or an episiotomy. Healing takes time. For women who had a cesarean, abdominal discomfort, back pain, and pelvic tension may still linger for weeks or months.

You might be afraid of pain or not trust your body again just yet. That fear itself can switch off arousal.

3. **Mental Load & Fatigue:**

Sleep deprivation, constant feeding, mental multitasking, and the invisible weight of motherhood can leave you drained. Add body image issues to the mix, and you've got a perfect recipe for "not tonight, not tomorrow either."

As my patient Neelam put it, "I love my husband deeply, but after putting my baby to sleep, I just want my bed — not romance."

This doesn't mean the love is gone. It means you need rest, reassurance, and realistic expectations.

### *"When can we have sex again?"*

Medically, most doctors say you can resume penetrative sex after 6 weeks — *if* there are no complications. But let me be very clear: just because you're cleared doesn't mean you're ready.

Think of that 6-week green light as a *starting point* for conversation, not a finish line for performance.

Many women wait 3–6 months, and some even longer. And that is perfectly okay.

Don't let movies or social media fool you. Nobody jumps back into sexy lingerie and passion like nothing happened. Most of us are in pyjamas with milk stains, trying to stay awake past 9 PM.

It takes time and effort. But more than anything, it takes honesty. With yourself, and with your partner.

### *"Is something wrong with my body?"*

Not necessarily. But if you're feeling persistent pain, severe dryness, a sense of aversion to touch, or complete numbness toward any sexual thought, it's worth checking in with your doctor. There are simple solutions:

- Vaginal lubricants or moisturisers
- Pelvic floor therapy (especially if there's pain or tightness)
- Topical estrogen creams (especially for breastfeeding moms with dryness)

Couples counselling, or sex therapy (for communication blocks or emotional trauma)

Don't suffer in silence. There is help.

### *"How can I rebuild sexual desire?"*

Start small. You don't need to "get it all back" at once.

Begin with non-sexual touch — a massage, spooning while watching TV, brushing each other's hair.

Create a "no pressure" zone — set aside time to be close without the expectation of intercourse.

Reignite the romance — leave little notes, plan a short coffee date, look into each other's eyes.

Remind yourself that your body, even if changed, is still capable of pleasure.

As one mom told me, "Once I stopped trying to 'go back' to how it was before the baby, and started focusing on what felt good now, everything changed."

### ❢ Take-home message:

*Desire after childbirth is complex — it's physical, emotional, and deeply personal.*

*There's no "right" time to resume sex. Only the time that feels right for you.*

*Low desire is common and treatable. Hormones, fatigue, and recovery all play a role.*

*Seek medical or therapeutic support if pain, fear, or emotional blocks persist.*

*You are not broken. You are healing. You are learning. And you are worthy of love and pleasure.*

## Contraception – Planning with Confidence

So, let's say you and your partner are slowly finding your rhythm again. The intimacy is returning — perhaps not exactly as it used to be, but in your own new, beautiful way. And then suddenly, it hits you:

"Wait… we're not ready for another baby. What if?"

This thought alone can trigger panic. Trust me, I've had mothers sit in my clinic with a crying baby in one arm, whispering in horror, "Doctor, I *cannot* get pregnant again right now."

You're not alone. And you do have options.

Let's talk contraception — openly, calmly, and without judgment. Because reclaiming your body also means reclaiming your choices.

"Do I even need contraception while breastfeeding?"

Ah, the famous myth:

"I'm breastfeeding. That means I can't get pregnant, right?"

Wrong… mostly.

Exclusively breastfeeding (meaning your baby is under six months, hasn't started solids, and you're feeding every 3-4 hours even at night) can suppress ovulation, a method known as the Lactational Amenorrhea Method (LAM).

But here's the catch:

LAM is only about 98% effective when done perfectly—and let's be honest, perfect conditions are rare in motherhood.

So yes, you *can* get pregnant while breastfeeding.

That's why it's important to use additional contraception if you're not ready for another baby.

### Choosing the Right Contraceptive: Your Options

Let's break it down. There's no one-size-fits-all, but understanding your choices can help you make an informed decision.

1. **Barrier Methods – Condoms (Male & Female)**

   ✓ No hormones, immediate protection, and also protects against infections.

   ✗ Can interrupt the moment, may reduce sensitivity.

Perfect for couples easing back into intimacy, especially when the mother isn't ready for hormonal methods yet.

2. **Hormonal Methods – Pills, Injections, Patches, Implants**

#### Mini-Pill (Progestin-only pill)

Safe during breastfeeding, taken daily.

#### Combined Oral Contraceptives (COCs)

Contains both estrogen and progestin. Wait at least 6 weeks postpartum, especially if not breastfeeding.

#### Injectables (like Depo-Provera)

One shot every 3 months. Convenient, effective.

### Implants (like Implanon/Nexplanon)

A thin rod under the skin of your arm works for 3 years.

✓ Highly effective, reversible.

✕ May cause spotting, mood changes, or weight fluctuation.

Many moms prefer the mini-pill or implant during breastfeeding. If you're unsure, ask your doctor for a postpartum-safe option.

**3. Intrauterine Devices (IUDs) – Copper or Hormonal (Mirena, Kyleena)**

Inserted into the uterus, lasts from 3 to 10 years.

**Copper IUD:** No hormones, may cause heavier periods.

**Hormonal IUD:** Lightens periods, reduces cramps.

✓ "Fit and forget." Very low maintenance, highly effective.

✕ Requires insertion by a doctor, may be uncomfortable for a day or two or longer for some women.

Many moms get an IUD inserted during their 6-week check-up. It's discreet and ideal for long-term spacing.

**4. Natural Methods – Fertility Awareness, Withdrawal**

These require tracking ovulation signs, menstrual cycles, and/or avoiding sex during fertile days.

✓ No hormones or devices.

✕ High failure rates if not practised perfectly.

Most doctors do not recommend this alone for postpartum contraception, especially since cycles can be irregular.

### 5. Permanent Methods – Tubal Ligation or Vasectomy

**Tubal Ligation:** A Surgical procedure to tie or seal the fallopian tubes.

**Vasectomy:** Male sterilisation; minor procedure, very effective.

✓ Permanent, highly effective.

✗ Only for couples sure they're done having children.

Some women choose tubal ligation during cesarean if they're sure. Otherwise, take your time to decide.

"What should I consider when choosing?"

Ask yourself:

Am I breastfeeding?

Do I want a hormone-free method?

Do I want something short-term or long-term?

How comfortable am I with pills or procedures?

What's my lifestyle like right now — can I remember a daily pill, or would I prefer something hands-free?

And most importantly: Have I discussed this with my partner and doctor?

"What if I don't want anything hormonal?"

That's valid. Some women have side effects with hormonal methods — mood swings, acne, weight gain, or headaches.

Non-hormonal options like copper IUDs, condoms, or natural methods may suit you better. Again, speak with a doctor to find what works best for *you*.

### Real Talk from Moms:

"I used condoms for the first year after my baby. It worked fine because we weren't super regular with sex anyway." – Meera, 33

"I got the Mirena IUD. It hurt a bit going in, but now I have zero period pain. I love it." – Diya, 29

"I told my husband, 'You get the vasectomy. I've done enough!' He agreed!" – Rhea, 37

### Take-home message:

*Don't wait until after you resume sex to think about contraception. Plan early.*

Discuss options with your doctor — especially if breastfeeding or having health concerns.

Choose what feels right for you—don't let pressure or fear make the decision.

Contraception is part of self-care. It lets you enjoy intimacy without the anxiety of an unexpected pregnancy.

## *Conclusion: Rebuilding Love, One Layer at a Time*

Rediscovering intimacy after childbirth is like tending a garden after a storm. Some flowers bloom easily, others take time. Some need extra care. Some never return the same way, but new beauty takes their place.

Your body has changed. Your relationship may have too. But intimacy can return — slowly, gently, joyfully.

Whether it's through a soft touch, a shared laugh, an honest conversation, or a quiet cuddle with no expectations… each moment brings you closer to your partner and yourself.

And when you're ready, emotionally and physically, the joy of sexual connection can return — on your terms, with confidence, without guilt.

You are allowed to want it, not want it, miss it, fear it, or welcome it.

There is no "normal." There is only *your* truth.

"Love is not just about sex. It's about presence, patience, and partnership."

You've already done the hardest thing — bringing life into the world. Now, it's time to give yourself permission to rediscover the joy of closeness, in all its forms.

## Chapter - 9

# Mindful Mothering

Mindful mothering isn't about being perfect. It's not about creating a Pinterest-worthy baby routine or maintaining calm every second of the day. It's about being *present* — truly present — with yourself, your child, and your experience of motherhood. It's about slowing down just enough to notice how you're feeling, what your body needs, and how your baby is communicating with you, even when they can't use words.

In the whirlwind of feeding schedules, sleepless nights, nappy changes, and unsolicited advice, mindfulness gives you a moment to breathe. It helps you pause before reacting, to listen instead of jumping to conclusions, to respond with empathy — toward your baby, and toward yourself.

Mindful mothering means being kind to yourself when the day doesn't go as planned. It's about creating space for joy, rest, and reflection. It's noticing when you're about to lose your temper and taking a step back. It's the small moments — sitting in silence with your baby sleeping on your chest, choosing to take a walk alone without guilt, or putting your phone away to just be with your child.

You don't have to be a yogi or a meditation expert. You just have to be willing to meet yourself exactly where you are, and to bring awareness, compassion, and acceptance into your daily life as a mother.

Because when you are more mindful, you are not only more attuned to your child — you also begin to reclaim a sense of calm and control that so often slips away during postpartum.

### *Mindfulness is awareness, not perfection*

The beauty of mindfulness is that it's not about doing everything right. It's about noticing when you're not okay and asking, "What do I need right now?" And then actually listening to the answer.

Maybe it's food. Maybe it's rest. Maybe it's silence. Maybe it's a connection.

Take a moment each day to check in with yourself. You can even set a daily alarm on your phone that says, "Hey, love, how are you really feeling today?"

Because when you are mindful of your needs, your limits, and your rhythms, you begin to show up as a fuller, more grounded version of yourself — for your baby, your family, and most importantly, for you.

As we walk through the different parts of this chapter, you'll see how mindfulness can show up in daily actions, how it can help reduce guilt, ease anxiety, and make motherhood more meaningful — on your terms.

## *Mindfulness in Daily Life – Eating, Drinking, Self-Care, and Boundaries:*

One of the biggest paradoxes of motherhood is that the more we pour into our children, the more we empty ourselves — unless we consciously choose to refill. And that refilling doesn't happen in grand vacations or deep spa retreats (although those are lovely when they happen). It begins in the smallest, most overlooked moments — like how we eat our food, drink our water, speak to ourselves, and hold space for our own well-being. This is where mindful mothering truly begins.

### Eat like you matter.

Let's start with something as basic and yet often ignored— eating.

I remember my early postpartum days with my daughter, Maanvi. Meals would often be cold by the time I got to them. Sometimes I'd eat standing, rocking her with one hand, shovelling bites into my mouth with the other. One day, my mother noticed and said gently, "Beta, your child will thrive if you thrive. Sit. Eat. You'll digest better. You'll feel better."

That hit home.

Mindful eating doesn't mean preparing a five-course meal with scented candles and Instagram-worthy plating. It simply means sitting down, even for five minutes, with your plate. Not scrolling through your phone. Not rushing through bites like it's a race. But chewing, tasting, and appreciating that meal — because your body just grew and birthed a human, and it needs nourishment and kindness.

If hot meals feel like a luxury, consider prepping some easy-to-grab healthy snacks — like soaked nuts, boiled eggs, fruit slices, or energy bars. And while we're here…

In your later journey during weight management, mindful eating would mean seeing what you are eating, eating the correct food at the correct time and in the correct quantity and avoiding dead foods or those foods which have only empty calories and no nutrition in your diet. That does not mean you don't indulge, you do, but mindfully.

### Drink like your body needs you.

Hydration is another act of self-care that often gets pushed aside. So many new moms walk around dizzy, lightheaded, and fatigued — not realising they're simply dehydrated. Especially if you're breastfeeding, your water needs are even higher.

Here's a tip: Keep a water bottle in all the places you sit most often — next to the bed, on the sofa, at your nursing chair. And every time you feed your baby, make it a cue to drink water yourself. It's a simple, mindful practice that not only supports your physical health but anchors you in the moment.

❢ Take-home message:

*Mindful eating and drinking are powerful, everyday self-care practices.*

*Mindfulness is not perfection; it's presence*

## Self-Care beyond the Basics – Reconnecting With Yourself and Others

You've probably heard this before, but it bears repeating: Self-care is not selfish. It's survival. It's sanity. Its strength. It's sacred.

But many of us carry deep-rooted guilt when we take time out for ourselves — especially when society applauds the "selfless mother" image.

Let's flip that narrative.

Self-care isn't about escaping your baby. It's about reconnecting with yourself. It could be five minutes of deep breathing. A short phone call with a friend. A long bath with your favourite playlist. Writing in a journal. A walk while someone else watches the baby. Whatever makes you feel a little more like you.

Priya, one of the mothers in my support group, once shared, "I'd spend all day attending to my twins, and by evening, I felt invisible. Then I started putting on a dab of kajal and perfume every morning — just for me. It shifted something. I felt seen."

That's the power of self-care — it helps you see yourself again.

When we talk about self-care, the image we have in mind is often reduced to the occasional salon visit or an uninterrupted shower. And while those are indeed precious luxuries in the postpartum world, true self-care goes far deeper. It's about reconnecting with who you are — not just as a mother, but as a whole woman. It's about tuning into your emotional and spiritual needs and remembering that your identity didn't dissolve when your baby was born. It just evolved.

Let's explore what deeper self-care looks like and why you should absolutely never feel guilty for embracing it.

## You Are More Than a Mother

It might sound obvious, but when you're knee-deep in diapers, burp cloths, and feeding schedules, it's easy to forget that you existed before motherhood — and that you still exist beyond it.

One evening, about six weeks after Maanvi was born, I caught my reflection in the mirror. My hair was unwashed, my kurta had milk stains, and I was sleepwalking through the day. I suddenly remembered how I used to start mornings with exercises and end nights reading a novel or painting something. I missed that version of myself. I missed *myself.*

That's when I made a pact with myself: ten minutes a day, just for me. Sometimes I painted. Sometimes I journaled. Other times, I just sat quietly and breathed. Those ten minutes weren't always peaceful — sometimes my baby cried in the background or I had to pause halfway — but those ten minutes reminded me: *I matter too.*

I had a mom who called me for a consultation, "It's been 18 months post my delivery, and I don't know what to do, where to start." My advice to her was to have a routine, have a bath, and get dressed . Such a basic thing was forgotten by that poor mother in the midst of the cyclone of responsibilities and confusion. However small it sounds, it did wonders for that mother, as it gave her a direction to begin. Something as small as getting dressed and having a routine for yourself can help in creating a rhythm in your journey.

### Reconnect Emotionally – With Yourself First

Your emotions after childbirth can feel like a rollercoaster — one minute you're glowing with joy, the next you're overwhelmed and teary. This is natural. Your hormones are shifting. Your life has transformed. But when you ignore those feelings, they bottle up, fester, and eventually explode.

Emotional self-care means creating space to feel. To grieve the old you, to celebrate the new you, and to process the fear, fatigue, and love that co-exist in this journey.

Start with something simple: naming your emotions. If you're exhausted, say it. If you're scared, admit it. If you're unsure, acknowledge it. Naming feelings gives them less power to control you and more space to be addressed.

You could write down your feelings, speak to a friend, or even voice-note yourself if writing feels like a chore. As one mom told me, "Sometimes I just say things out loud while feeding my baby. It's like talking to myself helps me unload, and I don't feel so heavy."

### Reconnect Spiritually – Finding Meaning in the Mess

Spiritual self-care doesn't have to be religious. It's about finding grounding and meaning in the midst of chaos. It could be prayer, meditation, listening to devotional songs, reading uplifting literature, or just sitting in silence.

For me, it was evening walks with Maanvi in the sling, as the sun set and the sky softened. That quiet time under the open sky felt like therapy. I didn't talk much. I just observed. The trees, the breeze, the tiny fingers of my baby curled into my kurta. That was spiritual healing.

Find what connects you to something bigger than your to-do list. It could be your faith, nature, art, or even a mantra that reminds you: This too shall pass.

### Reconnect Socially – Don't Mother Alone

Many women feel lonely after childbirth, even when surrounded by family. The emotional weight of motherhood can isolate you — especially when you feel like you're supposed to be grateful, happy, and coping all the time.

But here's the truth: you're allowed to need others. You're allowed to say, "I need help." And you deserve a village that supports you.

Call your friends. Even if it's just for five minutes to laugh about something silly. Join a mom support group— online or offline. Surround yourself with people who don't just ask about the baby, but also about you.

Neha, a mom I recently spoke to, said, "I used to feel bad about asking for help. Then one day, my sister came over and said, 'You're not meant to raise a child alone. Let me hold her while you nap.' I cried. Not because I was weak — but because I finally felt seen."

That's the power of connection.

### Guilt Is Not a Badge of Honour

Let's talk about the guilt that often shadows self-care. The voice that says, "If I step away from my baby, I'm a bad mom." Or "How can I enjoy a coffee with friends when the laundry is piling up?"

Here's what I want you to remember: A well-rested, emotionally grounded, spiritually connected mom is a better mom.

You're not abandoning your child when you care for yourself. You're modelling what healthy adulthood looks like. You're teaching your child that they, too, should grow up valuing their own well-being.

### Take-home message:

*Self-care is more than hygiene and sleep. It's about emotional, spiritual, and social well-being.*

You existed before motherhood, and reconnecting with that version of you is vital.

Create safe spaces to feel your emotions without judgment.

Spiritual self-care can ground you amidst postpartum chaos.

Asking for help and leaning on friends or family is not a weakness — it's wisdom.

Guilt has no place in self-care. You cannot pour from an empty cup

## *Boundaries are the new love language*

Motherhood is noisy. Not just from crying babies and constant demands, but also from the endless opinions, advice, and expectations hurled your way. "You should breastfeed." "Don't pick up the baby so much." "Why haven't you lost weight yet?"

You are allowed to say:

> "I don't want visitors today."
>
> "Please don't compare me to other moms."
>
> "I need 15 minutes to myself before I lose it."

Boundaries don't mean you're rude. They mean you're protecting your peace. And when you protect your peace, you mother from a place of calm, not chaos.

Motherhood has a way of dissolving the boundaries you once had. Suddenly, your time, body, sleep, and even personal space feel like public property — open to a baby's cries, relatives' advice, neighbours' curiosity, and social media's endless comparisons. But here's the thing: you need boundaries to thrive. They are not walls that isolate you — they are bridges that protect your well-being while still allowing healthy connection.

In this part, let's talk about the three big types of boundaries — emotional, physical, and social — and how setting them can change your postpartum life.

### Emotional Boundaries

Saying "I'm Not Okay" Without Shame

New moms are often expected to be glowing, grateful, and gung-ho about motherhood. But what if you're exhausted, sad, or just done for the day?

Setting emotional boundaries starts with owning your feelings and not apologising for them. It's okay to say:

> "I'm feeling overwhelmed right now."
>
> "I need some quiet time to process things."
>
> "Can we talk about this later? I'm too drained to think clearly right now."

A mom I know, Swati, shared how her well-meaning mother-in-law kept commenting on how she should be "strong like other mothers." It broke her. One day, she calmly said, "I'm strong in my own way. But even strong people need rest." That one sentence created a shift in the household — and gave her the space to breathe.

### 💡 Take-home message:

*You don't have to justify your emotions. You have the right to feel what you feel and to protect your mental space.*

### Physical Boundaries – Your Body, Your Rules

After childbirth, your body becomes a shared resource—held, touched, leaned on, often without warning. Breastfeeding, cuddling, postpartum recovery, visitors holding the baby — it can all feel like an invasion.

Setting physical boundaries means reclaiming your body, piece by piece. You can:

Ask for privacy when feeding or resting.

Say no to visitors if you're not feeling up to it.

Choose how and when to engage in intimacy again with your partner.

One mother, Anjali, told me she locked the bathroom door for the first time in months and took a 15-minute bath while her husband watched their baby. "I felt like a queen," she laughed. "Not because of the bath, but because I chose to claim that time and space for myself."

### 💡 Take-home message:

*Your body is still yours. Let yourself heal on your terms, without guilt.*

### Social Boundaries – Managing People and Opinions

If there's one thing motherhood brings in abundance — other than love and laundry — it's unsolicited advice.

From relatives, neighbours, the aunty next door, Instagram influencers, and sometimes even strangers in the elevator.

Creating social boundaries means deciding whose voice you will allow into your sacred space.

### Start by asking yourself:

Does this person's opinion help me or drain me?

Do I feel judged or supported after I talk to them?

Do I owe them my time or attention right now?

You don't have to explain your choices to everyone. Whether it's choosing formula over breastfeeding, sleep training your baby, or deciding not to attend a function— your reasons are yours.

A lovely mother named Kavita told me how she simply replied, "Thank you, I'll consider that," to every piece of advice she didn't agree with. That one sentence helped her stay polite without getting pulled into debates or guilt spirals.

### Take-home message:

*Not every voice deserves your attention. Curate your circle to include those who support, not sabotage, your peace.*

### You're Not Being Rude. You're Being Real.

One of the biggest fears mothers have when creating boundaries is: *Will I seem rude?* But let me reassure you— setting boundaries is an act of love, not defiance.

You're saying:

> "I love you, but I need space."
>
> "I value this relationship, but I must protect my mental health."
>
> "I want to enjoy this phase, but I need rest and respect to do that."

Practical Tips for Setting Boundaries:

Start small. You don't have to overhaul your life in a day. Choose one situation where you feel stretched and speak up there.

Use "I" statements. Say, "I need some time to rest now," instead of, "You're making me tired." It feels less confrontational and more honest.

Be consistent. Boundaries are effective when reinforced gently but firmly over time.

Know your rights. You're allowed to say no. To rest. To take a break. To ask for help.

### ❢ Take-home message:

*Boundaries are not selfish — they're self-respect in action.*

*Emotional boundaries help you protect your feelings and communicate them without guilt.*

*Physical boundaries allow you to reclaim your space and body in a loving way.*

*Social boundaries help you filter out unhelpful noise and focus on what truly matters.*

*Saying "no" doesn't make you rude — it makes you real.*

## Who Really Matters – The Art of Saying No with Grace

Motherhood is like opening your doors wide — to love, to chaos, to sleepless nights, to unsolicited advice, and to a thousand expectations. And in the middle of all this, you may find yourself wondering, "Where did *I* go?" It's easy to get lost in the noise of people, obligations, and a never-ending to-do list. That's why this part is all about something powerful: learning who really matters — and how to say no to everything else.

Let's be honest. Most mothers are people pleasers. We're wired to care, to nurture, to keep the peace. But motherhood demands that we choose wisely where we spend our energy — because it's already stretched thin. So let's talk about how to tune out what doesn't serve you and lean into what truly does.

### Whose Voice Counts?

In the age of Instagram stories, family WhatsApp groups, parenting blogs, and friendly-but-nosy neighbours, it's hard to figure out whose opinion to listen to. Here's a gentle rule of thumb: Listen to people who love you *and* respect your choices.

One mother I worked with, Riya, shared how her aunt constantly criticised her for not oiling the baby's head daily or using "chemical diapers." At first, Riya tried to explain. But over time, she realised that this aunt wasn't open to learning — just judging. She made a quiet decision: "I stopped sharing details with her. I smiled, nodded, and then went on with what I knew was right for me and my baby."

And that's key — you don't need to convince everyone. The people who truly matter — your partner, your inner circle, your trusted doctor — *they'll get it*. They'll ask how you are, not just how the baby is. They'll offer support, not judgement.

### Letting Go of Obligations that Drain You

There's a cultural narrative, especially in Indian homes, that mothers must say yes to everything:

> "Come to the pooja, it's just for two hours!"
>
> "Why didn't you attend the wedding? It looks bad."
>
> "It's your duty to host the guests."

But guess what? You are allowed to say no.

You are not being disrespectful when you protect your energy. You are being wise.

Take the example of Meenal, a new mom who skipped a family get-together that clashed with her baby's nap schedule. "At first, I felt guilty," she told me. "But then I reminded myself — I'm not saying no to family, I'm saying yes to my baby's peace and my own sanity."

**Take-home message:**

*The world will adjust. Your baby's routine, your rest, your emotional bandwidth — they matter more than appearances.*

## Saying No with Grace (Not Guilt)

We think saying no has to be loud or rude. It doesn't. You can be firm *and* kind. Here are a few gentle ways to say no:

> "I'm not up for that right now, but thank you for thinking of me."

> "We're focusing on rest and bonding, so we'll skip this event."

> "I'll let you know if I can manage that later, but I can't commit right now."

And sometimes, no explanation is needed at all. A simple, "Not this time," is perfectly valid.

## Saying No to Yourself

Let's not forget the hardest person to say no to — yourself. The inner voice that pushes you to do more, be more, and never take a break. The voice that says:

> "You haven't cleaned the house in days!"

> "Other moms are already back at work. What's wrong with you?"

> "You should be able to do this without help."

That voice? It doesn't get a seat at your table anymore.

You are allowed to be tired.

You are allowed to take your time.

You are allowed to say, "This is enough for today."

Start by noticing these inner pressures. Write them down if you have to. Then challenge them with compassion.

One mom, Preeti, started a little ritual. Every night before bed, she asked herself, "Did I do my best with what I had today?" If the answer was yes, she let everything else go. That's mindfulness in action.

Who Really Matters? A Simple Exercise

Here's a small activity you can try:

1. Take a piece of paper and draw three circles — like a target.
2. In the innermost circle, write the names of people who love and support you unconditionally.
3. In the middle circle, list those whose opinions matter *sometimes* — extended family, certain friends, etc.
4. In the outer circle, write down the noise — social media, distant relatives, society at large.

Now, every time you feel overwhelmed by someone's opinion, ask yourself: *Which circle are they in?* If they're not in the centre, maybe their voice doesn't deserve that much power in your decisions.

💡 Take-home message:

*Your energy is limited. Spend it on people and tasks that nourish you, not drain you.*

*You don't owe everyone an explanation. No is a complete sentence.*

*Saying no is not rejection — it's redirection towards what matters more.*

*Don't forget to silence your inner critic, too. You deserve your own kindness.*

*Your peace is worth protecting — even if it means disappointing a few people*

## The Comparison Trap – You vs. Other Moms, Your First-Time Mom Self, and Everyone in Between

It starts innocently enough.

You see a post of your friend doing yoga at 6 weeks postpartum, and think, *"She's already back in shape."*

Your neighbour boasts, "My baby slept through the night by 2 months," and you wonder, *"What am I doing wrong?"*

You scroll past a mom's artfully arranged snack tray and feel inadequate as you hand your toddler a banana for the third time that day.

And just like that, you've fallen into the comparison trap.

It's subtle. It's sneaky. And it's absolutely draining.

### Why Do We Compare?

Because we care. Because we want to do a good job. Because we've been conditioned to look outward for validation.

And sometimes, we don't even need social media or relatives to trigger us. We compare ourselves… to ourselves.

"I handled things so well with my first baby — why am I struggling now?"

"I used to have more energy, more patience, a better routine. What happened?"

You've changed. Your life has changed. Your baby is not the same as your last one. And you, dear mama, are not a robot — you're a human, evolving with every experience.

### Real-Life Stories: When Comparison Creeps In

Shalini, a second-time mom, shared, "With my first baby, I was so organised. I had the steriliser, the schedules, the milestone charts. Now, with my second, I feel like I'm constantly behind. I started doubting myself."

After talking it through, she realised her expectations hadn't adapted to her current reality — two kids, a part-time job, ageing parents at home. Once she permitted herself to be a different kind of mother this time, not a lesser one, her confidence returned.

Then there's Ayesha, who couldn't stop comparing herself to her college friend who seemed to have it all — fit body, clean house, adorable twins. "But when I met her in person," Ayesha said, "she opened up about feeling isolated and battling anxiety. It was a wake-up call — we're all struggling in our own ways."

### The Cost of Comparison...

Comparison rarely motivates. More often, it paralyses.

It whispers:

> "You're not enough."
>
> "You're behind."
>
> "You're failing."

And it distracts you from the one thing that matters — your own unique journey.

Here's the truth: That mom you're admiring? She probably envies something about you, too. Maybe it's your patience. Your bond with your baby. Your sense of humour. We all have different strengths, different struggles.

### What You Can Do Instead?

**Name It When It Happens**

Catch yourself mid-thought. "I'm comparing again." Just saying it out loud creates awareness and breaks the spiral.

**Curate Your Social Media**

Unfollow or mute accounts that make you feel inadequate. Follow real, honest, diverse motherhood content. Or take a break altogether.

**Talk About It**

Say it to a friend: "I feel like I'm not doing enough." Chances are, she'll say, "Me too." And suddenly, you'll both feel less alone.

### Celebrate Small Wins

Did you make it through a tough day without yelling? That's growth. Did you shower *and* eat today? You're doing amazing. Make your own checklist, and let it reflect what actually matters to you.

### Remember, No One Posts the Full Story

That curated reel you saw of a mom happily playing with her baby on a picnic blanket? You didn't see the 3 tantrums, spilt juice, and the 40 minutes it took to leave the house. Real life is messy — and beautiful in its messiness.

### Take-Home Quotes:

> "Comparison is the thief of joy." – Theodore Roosevelt

> "Don't compare your behind-the-scenes to someone else's highlight reel."

### A Journal Prompt for You:

Take a few minutes tonight to write down:

One thing you admire about your own mothering style

One area where you've grown since becoming a mom

One thing that's uniquely yours — your superpower as a mom

Keep this somewhere you can revisit on hard days.

**Take-home message:**

*Comparison can sneak in from anywhere — other moms, social media, even your past self.*

*It drains your joy and disconnects you from your own journey.*

*Awareness, community, and self-compassion are your tools to fight it.*

*You are not here to win at motherhood. You're here to experience it — fully, imperfectly, and honestly.*

## The Myth of the Perfect Mother – And the Guilt That Follows

"Am I doing it right?"

It's the one question that quietly echoes in the minds of mothers everywhere. Whether you're nursing at 3 a.m., watching your toddler throw a meltdown in the middle of a grocery store, or just lying in bed scrolling through yet another Instagram reel of a mom who "has it all together", — that doubt creeps in.

It's a haunting whisper, sometimes a roar:

"Am I enough?"

Welcome to the exhausting and unrelenting pressure of being a "perfect mother."

Where Does This Pressure Come From?

Sometimes it's society.

Sometimes it's your own upbringing.

Sometimes it's that voice inside your head that's trying so hard to do what's "right" for your baby.

You may have grown up watching your mom sacrifice everything, never complain, always have a clean home, and cook three fresh meals a day. Or perhaps you were raised hearing "good mothers don't get angry," "good mothers breastfeed for two years," "good mothers never need help."

Then, there's modern parenting culture — an overwhelming mix of advice, judgment, and curated perfection that leaves very little room for error or emotional honesty.

### Real-Life Snapshots of Guilt

Ritika, a paediatrician herself, broke down one evening because she gave her daughter a screen for 30 minutes just to finish some work. "I knew logically it was okay, but emotionally, I felt like I'd failed her," she confessed. "That guilt stayed with me for days."

Then there's Meera, a stay-at-home mom who struggled with rage after her second baby. "I'd yell, then cry, then feel terrible. And then feel guilty for making it about me. Isn't this supposed to be the happiest time of my life?"

But the truth is, these struggles are not signs of failure. They're signs of being human. Of loving deeply and feeling overwhelmed. Of trying to give your child the best of you, and wondering if you still know who "you" even are.

## Let's Talk About That Guilt.

Mother guilt is sneaky. It shows up even when you're doing your best.

> You feel guilty for working and leaving your baby.
>
> You feel guilty for staying home and not "using your degree."
>
> You feel guilty for snapping at your partner.
>
> You feel guilty for needing space.
>
> You even feel guilty when you enjoy time away from your kids.

The guilt is endless because the standards are impossible.

As one mother said, "You're expected to parent like you don't work, and work like you don't parent."

## Reframing Perfection...

Perfect doesn't exist. And it certainly doesn't exist in parenting.

What does exist is:

> Showing up, again and again, even when you're exhausted.
>
> Apologising and repairing after you've lost your cool.
>
> Loving your child fiercely, even on days you don't feel very lovable yourself.

That's not just good enough. That's extraordinary.

What You Can Do Instead?

**Redefine Success**

Not everything has to be picture-perfect. Maybe your toddler didn't eat all the veggies today — but did you make them laugh? Did you share a cuddle? That counts.

**Own Your Emotions**

Guilt thrives in silence. Talk about it. Write about it. Let it out. You don't have to carry it alone.

**Set Realistic Expectations**

You are one person. You cannot meet every need all the time. And you don't have to. A happy mom matters more than a perfect routine.

**Practice Self-Compassion**

Would you speak to your best friend the way you speak to yourself? If not, it's time to change the tone of your inner dialogue.

Take-Home Quote:

***"There's no way to be a perfect mother, but a million ways to be a good one."***

**– Jill Churchill**

A Gentle Exercise

Tonight, write a list of 5 things you did right today. No matter how small.

Even if it's:

I smiled at my baby.

I made it through the day.

I asked for help.

Celebrate yourself, mama. You deserve it.

❢ Take-home message:

*The pressure to be perfect creates guilt and burnout.*

*Comparison and unrealistic standards only add fuel to the fire.*

*Reframing expectations, speaking your truth, and practising kindness toward yourself are the antidotes.*

*Remember, your child doesn't need a perfect mom — they need a real, present and a loving one.*

### The Invisible Load – The Mental Work No One Sees

You know that moment when you're lying in bed, but your mind is wide awake?

You're not thinking about a spa day or planning a vacation. Instead, you're ticking through a never-ending mental checklist:

Buy more diapers.

Did I send that message to the paediatrician?

What's in the fridge for tomorrow's lunchbox?

Oh no, we're out of detergent again.

I forgot to RSVP to that birthday party!

This, my dear, is the invisible load — the unseen, unacknowledged, and unrelenting mental labour that most mothers carry.

### What Is the Invisible Load?

It's not just about doing things. It's about thinking about them, planning for them, and remembering them — over and over again.

It includes:

Keeping track of appointments, vaccinations, and school events.

Knowing where every sock, pacifier, and favourite toy is at any given time.

Anticipating your child's needs before they even ask.

Remembering to call your in-laws, plan for festivals, pack snacks, and so on.

It's the full-time mental project management that keeps the household — and often, the family — running.

Real-Life Snapshots

Aditi, a software engineer, once told me, "My husband helps with the baby, but he waits to be told what to do. I have to remember everything — then delegate, then follow up. It's easier to just do it myself."

Sound familiar?

Another mom, Shreya, laughed as she said, "When my toddler has a fever, I immediately think about paracetamol dosage, doctor's number, cancelling meetings, meal prep, sleep disruptions, laundry… My husband just says, 'Poor baby, let's see how she is in the morning.'"

This isn't to say men don't help or don't care. Many do. But the mental burden — the constant vigilance — often defaults to the mother.

Why Is It Exhausting?

Because it's relentless. It doesn't end at 5 p.m. or on weekends. You can be sitting with your child and still mentally multitasking. Over time, this leads to:

Mental fatigue

Emotional burnout

Resentment

Disconnection from your own needs

And worst of all? Many mothers feel guilty about asking for help. As if needing help means you're not strong enough.

So, What Can We Do?

**1. Name It**

Start by acknowledging that this is real work — even if it's invisible. Give yourself credit for the thinking, organising, and anticipating you do all day long.

**2. Delegate the Responsibility, Not Just the Task**

Don't just say "Can you make lunch?"

**Say:** "Can you take over weekday lunch prep completely this month? That includes planning, shopping, and packing."

Let your partner own the task *end-to-end*. The mental work needs to be shared, too.

3. **Use Tools**

    Shared digital calendars

    Family whiteboards

    To-do list apps

These aren't magic, but they help shift some of the weight outside your head.

4. **Have Regular Check-Ins**

Set aside 15 minutes weekly with your partner to go over the upcoming week's needs. Make it collaborative, not nagging.

A Real-Life Turnaround

Rina, a mom of two, started something she called the "Mental Load Monday" with her husband. Every Monday morning, over coffee, they split up school drop-offs, grocery shopping, and chores. "It's not perfect," she says, "but just being seen and heard has made a huge difference."

A Gentle Reminder

You don't have to carry everything.

You don't have to remember everything.

You are allowed to rest, to forget, to ask.

Being a good mother doesn't mean being superhuman. It means being real. And being real means recognizing when you're overloaded — and letting some of it go.

### Take-Home Quote:

***"Just because you can do it all doesn't mean You should."***

**— Unknown**

### 💡 Take-home message:

*The invisible load is the constant mental work mothers do that often goes unnoticed.*

*It's emotionally and mentally exhausting.*

*Naming it, sharing responsibility, and using planning tools can help lighten the burden.*

*Regular communication with your partner is key to sustainable support.*

## *Task Stratification – Doing What Matters and Leaving the Rest*

Let's play a quick game.

You have:

A pile of laundry waiting to be folded

A cranky baby on your hip

An unanswered work email

A family WhatsApp group buzzing with "Are you coming for dinner?"

And your stomach is growling because you skipped lunch (again)

What do you do first?

This, my friend, is where task stratification comes in. It's the gentle art of sorting, prioritising, and letting go — without the guilt. It's what allows you to move from chaos to clarity, even when you're knee-deep in the thick of motherhood.

## What Is Task Stratification?

Task stratification is the process of breaking down your tasks, ranking them by urgency and importance, and then deciding what needs to be:

Done now

Delegated

Delayed

Dropped altogether

It's not about doing everything — it's about doing the right things at the right time, with kindness to yourself.

The Why behind It

Motherhood often feels like a full inbox. The mental load (remember Part 7?) and emotional labour combine to make everything seem urgent. But when everything feels urgent, nothing truly gets your full attention — least of all you.

When you learn to stratify, you free yourself from:

- Guilt over the dishes in the sink
- Pressure to reply to every message instantly

The belief that your home must look "Insta-worthy" to be a happy one

### A Real-Life Story

Megha, a first-time mom and teacher, once shared, "I used to think I had to do everything — pump milk, prepare meals, keep the house tidy, stay in touch with friends. I was constantly overwhelmed. Then I started making a simple 'Must-Do / Nice-to-Do' list every morning."

She smiled and added, "Now, I focus on three essential things a day. If the rest gets done, great. If not, I let it go."

### How to Stratify Tasks (Without Losing Your Mind)

**1. List It Out**

Take five minutes to brain-dump everything on your mind. Everything from "cut baby's nails" to "schedule dental checkup" to "take a nap."

**2. Label It**

For each task, ask yourself:

Is it urgent or important?

Can someone else do it?

Will it still matter next week?

Use simple labels:

NOW – urgent and important

LATER – important but not urgent

DELEGATE – someone else can handle it

DROP – not worth your time or energy

**3. Be Ruthless with the "Drop" List**

You don't have to say yes to every outing, video call, or elaborate meal plan. A clean kitchen can wait. A rested mom is more valuable than a spotless floor.

**4. Protect Your "Non-Negotiables"**

These are your daily anchors — your 20-minute walk, quiet coffee, journaling, reading, whatever helps you feel human. Guard them.

Gentle Tips That Help.

Use visual planners or Post-it notes — seeing your tasks makes them feel less overwhelming.

Time block — assign chunks of time for similar tasks to reduce decision fatigue.

Plan your energy, not just your time — don't schedule high-focus tasks when you know you'll be tired or cranky.

Accept "good enough" — perfection is often the enemy of peace.

A Quote to Carry with You:

***"You can do anything, but not everything."***

**— David Allen**

Include Your Partner in the Process

Stratification works best when shared. Once a week, sit down with your partner and divide the load realistically. Ask:

What tasks drain you?

What tasks do you enjoy?

What can be outsourced, even occasionally?

Let your spouse handle entire areas — like school coordination, diaper restocking, or Sunday meal prep. Not just the execution, but the thinking and remembering too.

## Final Thoughts

You are not lazy for not doing everything. You are wise for knowing what matters most.

Motherhood is not a checklist. It's a relationship. It's okay if the floor isn't mopped today. If your child is hugged, heard, and held, you're already doing more than enough.

### 💡 Take-home message:

*Task stratification is about sorting and prioritising tasks so you can focus on what matters.*

*Break your list into: Do Now, Do Later, Delegate, and Drop.*

*Protect your energy and include your partner in planning and execution.*

*Let go of perfection and permit yourself to rest*

Motherhood isn't a race to be run or a mountain to be conquered. It's a rhythm — a flow of love, presence, and learning to show up imperfectly but wholeheartedly. As you move through sleepless nights, sticky fingers, and whispered lullabies, may you carry this one truth with you: your worth is not measured by how much you do, but by how deeply you love — your baby, your people, and most importantly yourself. Mindful mothering isn't about having it all together. It's about coming home to yourself, again and again, even in the mess. Especially in the mess. You're doing better than you think. And you're never alone on this journey.

## Chapter - 10

# Redefining You - Thriving, Not Just Surviving

There's a peculiar silence that follows after the flurry of postpartum visits, feeding struggles, and sleepless nights begin to settle. A silence that mothers often sit with in the quiet of the afternoon nap time or in the few moments stolen in the shower. That silence is where a question echoes: *"Who am I now?"*

It's a question I've asked myself, and one I've heard countless women whisper across the clinic table. The journey of motherhood is not just about giving birth to a child — it's also about rebirthing ourselves. And yet, this part is rarely talked about.

One of my patients, Ayesha, a spirited classical dancer, once told me, "I haven't touched my ghungroos in over a year. I feel like that version of me doesn't exist anymore." It wasn't the loss of a hobby — it was the erosion of self.

❢ Take-home message:

*You don't lose yourself in motherhood. You just take a detour — sometimes messy, sometimes magical — to rediscover who you are.*

When we become mothers, we're flooded with responsibilities, routines, and expectations. Suddenly, the "you" who reads poetry, paints on weekends, or laughs freely with friends feels distant. Society doesn't help — mothers are applauded for sacrifice, not for self-care.

Let me tell you about Radhika, a once-passionate graphic designer who had taken a two-year break after her baby. When she came to see me, she was exhausted and quietly angry. "I love my son," she said, "but I hate that I feel invisible." She hadn't had a haircut in a year. Her days blurred into bottles, naps, and endless chores. "Even my husband calls me 'mumma' now. It's like I've become a utility."

We spent time together exploring what Radhika missed. She wasn't ready to go back to full-time work, but she started freelancing during her baby's nap times. Her confidence soared. "Even just knowing that I could still design — that I had ideas — gave me back my spark," she said.

💡 Take-home message:

*Your dreams and desires don't expire when you become a mother. They evolve — and they're still valid.*

The moment a baby is born, so is a mother. But what often gets missed is the quiet, personal rebirth of the woman herself. Amidst nappies and night feeds, she often disappears — until she starts looking for herself again.

You've probably heard the phrase "just surviving" more times than you can count. Surviving on three hours of sleep. Surviving on reheated chai and leftovers. Surviving through cluster feeds, diaper blowouts, emotional breakdowns — yours and your baby's.

But at some point, that fog begins to lift. And you deserve more than survival. You deserve to thrive. This chapter is about that journey — about rediscovering who you are, what you love, and how to build a life that feels full again.

You are not just a caregiver. You are a whole person with needs, desires, and ambitions that still matter. This chapter may feel repetitive, but it's more aligned with your journey in redefining yourself.

## The Identity Shift That No One Warns You About

### Let's start with the reality

Motherhood changes you. Emotionally. Physically. Socially. You might look in the mirror and not recognise the woman staring back.

The identity shift is one of the deepest parts of postpartum life. You might feel like you're now expected to be only one thing: “Mummy.” But the truth is, you’re still a daughter, a friend, a partner, a professional, a woman with her own needs.

This emotional duality can be difficult. We feel guilty for wanting time away, for enjoying a cup of coffee alone, for pursuing goals that aren’t centred around our child. But guilt shouldn’t be a measuring stick for love.

I often suggest to mothers: Make a list of five things you used to love doing — big or small. Reading fiction, going for walks, wearing lipstick, playing a sport, and watching K-dramas. Then pick one and find a way to do it once a week.

Shalini, a new mom I saw recently, began going for early morning walks while her husband watched the baby. She’d grab a chai from the local tapri, plug in her music, and just breathe. “It sounds silly,” she told me, “but I started looking forward to mornings again.”

Before her baby, Ananya was a project manager leading teams across time zones. After her baby, she said, “I felt invisible. Everyone asked about the baby. No one asked how I was.” That feeling — of being needed but not seen— is incredibly common.

Rediscovering your identity doesn’t mean going back to who you were. It means becoming someone new who honours her past while embracing the now.

Start by asking:

What do I miss from my old life?

What brings me joy right now?

What do I need more of?

Meera, a classical dancer, stopped practicing after childbirth. "I felt guilty even humming a song," she said. Her turning point came when her toddler swayed to music from the kitchen. "It reminded me that my love for dance is part of what makes me a good mother." She started dancing again — 10 minutes a day. "It saved me."

Take-home message:

*Tiny actions that honour your joy are how you start thriving. Small rituals that nourish you can become your anchors.*

### *Long-Term Well-Being: Building the Foundation*

Thriving doesn't mean doing more. It means doing what fills you up. Here are four anchors:

**1. Mental Health Support**

Sana kept her struggles to herself. "Everyone around me looked like they had it all together," she said. Only after a friend admitted she was in therapy did Sana seek help. "That first session? I cried through it. But I came out lighter."

**2. Physical Health**

Sneha, a mom of twins, committed to walking every evening — even if just 15 minutes. "It wasn't about fitness. It was about feeling like I was in my body again."

### 3. Purpose and Passion

Charu used to paint. She joined a virtual art challenge and painted one postcard a week. "It gave me something to look forward to besides bottles and burp cloths."

### 4. Boundaries

Neelam started saying no to phone calls after 9 PM — even from family. "Those 30 minutes before bed were mine — to journal, sip warm water, and breathe."

💡 Take-home message:

*Thriving needs a plan. Build it one habit at a time.*

## Shifting from "Should" to "Want"

Ritika's day was ruled by shoulds — "I should cook from scratch," "I should take my baby to the park daily." She was constantly exhausted.

One day, she asked herself, "Who said I should?" She began making choices based on what felt right. Some days she cooked, some days they ordered in. "That shift changed everything. I started feeling like I was living — not performing."

💡 Take-home message:

*Let go of the 'shoulds'. Lean into what feels aligned.*

## Rediscovering Mental and Emotional Balance

Reclaiming your identity after becoming a mother isn't just about getting back to the old "you." It's about discovering a new version of yourself that encompasses both the mother you've become and the woman you were before. This journey is often emotional and mental—it requires you to navigate the guilt, self-doubt, and societal pressures that come with the territory of motherhood.

When I had my first child, I felt a similar disconnect. The demands of being a new mom were relentless, and for a while, I didn't know how to fit myself into the picture. I remember missing the quiet moments I used to spend reading or journaling, and I felt overwhelmed by the constant demands. But as time passed, I realised that I needed to carve out time for myself, even in small ways. Whether it was reading a chapter of a book before bed or taking a walk around the block, these little moments helped me reconnect with myself.

Take-home message:

*Reclaiming your identity requires self-awareness and self-compassion. It's okay to acknowledge that you need time for yourself.*

Mental health plays a crucial role in this process. Many mothers experience what's often referred to as "identity loss" after having children. It's natural to feel like your life has changed in ways you didn't anticipate, and it's easy to feel like your identity has been overtaken by the role of mother. However, it's important to remember that taking care of yourself mentally and emotionally isn't selfish — it's necessary. Your mental well-being forms the foundation of your ability to care for others.

## *Embracing Hobbies and Passions and Rekindling Ambition Again*

"I felt torn," said Pooja, an HR executive. "Wanting to go back to work felt like betrayal." But six months in, her mother asked gently, "Why are you punishing yourself for wanting more?" That was her wake-up call. She returned to work part-time and felt renewed. "I come back home ready to give, not drained."

Whether it's work, study, writing, or entrepreneurship — your ambition is part of who you are. So many mothers ask, "Is it okay if I want more?" More than just motherhood?

Yes, a hundred times yes.

Wanting a career, a creative life, financial independence, a second degree — whatever it is — doesn't make you less devoted. It just makes you human. You are allowed to expand, even as you nurture.

As Dr Shraddha Sanghani (yes, that's me — doctor, mother, writer) often says, "Don't shrink your world to fit others' comfort. Grow it to fit your soul."

Take-home message:

*Your growth doesn't threaten your love for your child. It reflects it. You're modelling strength, joy, and purpose. Your child needs a happy, fulfilled you. Not a burnt-out, self-erased one.*

One of the most powerful ways to rediscover yourself is through your hobbies and passions. Before motherhood, you may have loved reading, painting, yoga, or dancing— whatever your passions were, they were a big part of your identity. But often, these get pushed aside in the whirlwind of motherhood. The problem is, if you don't give yourself the time and space to enjoy these things, you may begin to feel like you've lost touch with who you are.

Take-home message:

*Rediscovering your passions is not just a luxury — it's a necessity for your mental and emotional well-being.*

I had a conversation with my patient, Shalini, who loved photography before becoming a mother. "I used to spend hours with my camera, capturing moments in nature. It felt like part of me was missing when I couldn't do that anymore," she said. So, Shalini decided to make photography a priority again. She set aside an hour every Sunday morning for herself, leaving her husband in charge of the kids. It didn't matter that it was just an hour — she came back feeling more like herself. That one hour, away from the demands of motherhood, allowed her to reconnect with her creative side.

Take-home message:

*Small amounts of time dedicated to your hobbies can help you rediscover the passions that once defined you.*

### Body Image and Self-Confidence

Another area where mothers often feel the pressure to change is in their body image. Pregnancy and childbirth change your body in profound ways no one prepares for, and it's natural to feel disconnected from the body you once knew. But it's important to remember that these changes are part of your story — they represent the strength and resilience it took to carry and nurture your child.

I remember standing in front of the mirror two weeks after delivery, holding my belly, and wondering if it would ever feel like mine again. As a doctor, I knew the science. But as a woman, I still felt a pang.

Suhana, a banker and new mom, once told me with tears in her eyes, "I don't feel sexy anymore. I don't even feel like a woman — just a caretaker."

These feelings are real. But here's what I tell every mother: Your body just created life. It deserves gratitude before judgment. That doesn't mean you shouldn't want to feel fit or beautiful again — it means your motivation should come from self-love, not self-loathing.

Start slow. Begin with light movement — walking, gentle yoga, pelvic floor exercises. Rebuild strength from the inside out. Eat to nourish, not to punish.

### 💡 Take-home message:

*You don't need to "bounce back." You need to "move forward" at your own pace — with kindness.*

*Your body is a testament to your strength and resilience.*

I had a conversation with Priya, who had struggled with her post-pregnancy body. She confided, "I look in the mirror and don't recognise myself anymore. I feel like I'm carrying all this extra weight, and I just don't feel confident."

I gently reminded her that the body she was seeing was the same body that gave life to her baby. "You've created a human being," I told her, "and that is something incredibly powerful."

It's essential to work toward self-love and acceptance during this phase. Fitness goals should come from a place of self-care, not self-criticism. Reclaiming your body doesn't mean focusing solely on weight loss or fitting into your pre-pregnancy jeans; it means reconnecting with your body and showing it the love and care it deserves.

**Take-home message:**

*Focus on self-care and self-love, not unrealistic beauty standards. Your body is beautiful, just as it is.*

## Nurturing Friendships and Social Connections

Another important aspect of reclaiming your identity is nurturing your friendships and social connections. Before motherhood, you probably spent time with friends, went out for coffee dates, or attended social events. However, once the baby arrives, these friendships often take a backseat.

But social connection is vital for mental and emotional health. It's easy to become isolated when you're home with a newborn, and it's important to carve out time to nurture your friendships.

Your friends without kids might not understand why you've disappeared. Your mom friends might only talk about sleep schedules. Somewhere in the middle, you might crave connection but not know how to reach out.

Push past the hesitation. Send that text. Ask someone to drop by. Accept help. And if your friends don't get it, find new ones who do. Join local mom groups or online communities. There's always someone else searching for connection, too.

💡 Take-home message:

*You weren't meant to mother alone. Your social self-matters just as much as your maternal one.*

I had a conversation with Nisha, who had recently become a mother. "I feel like I've lost touch with everyone," she admitted. "I used to meet my friends for coffee every week, but now I'm just focused on the baby."

Together, we brainstormed ways for Nisha to reconnect with her friends. She started by scheduling regular meetups with her close friends, even if it was just for an hour or two. These moments helped her feel more grounded and reminded her that she was still Nisha — the woman with her own life, interests, and passions.

💡 Take-home message:

*Make time for your friendships, even if it's just a quick phone call or a coffee date. These relationships are vital for your sense of self. They were part of your identity before, and they will continue to be a part of your life ahead.*

What about relationships?

Motherhood can sometimes distance us from our partners. You're both navigating new roles, and often, romance takes a back seat. But this stage, too, can be navigated with intention.

I encourage couples to have honest check-ins — not just about the baby, but about each other. What do you miss? What do you need? Even small acts — holding hands, leaving a kind note, watching a show together — can restore connection.

Ritu and Arjun, first-time parents, made a pact to do "Friday chai nights" after putting the baby to bed. They'd talk, not about poop schedules or feeding charts, but about books, memories, and dreams. "It reminded us," Ritu said, "that we're still us."

Take-home message:

*You're not just co-parents. You're partners. Nurture that bond, even in five-minute windows.*

### Carving Time for Yourself

As a mother, it's easy to get caught up in the demands of caring for your children, your spouse, and your home. But one of the most important things you can do for yourself is carve out time for yourself, even if it's just a few minutes each day. Whether it's a walk around the block, reading a book, or enjoying a bath, these moments allow you to recharge.

Take-home message:

*It's okay to take time for yourself. You can't pour from an empty cup.*

I remember a patient of mine, Sanya, who struggled with guilt about taking time for herself. "I feel like I'm always putting myself last," she said. "But when I try to do something for myself, I feel like I'm neglecting my baby."

Sanya eventually made a pact with her husband. They would take turns looking after the baby so each of them could get some personal time. Sanya started with small moments — five minutes of deep breathing, 15 minutes of reading. Eventually, those small moments turned into bigger, more regular breaks. Sanya started to feel like herself again. Her confidence grew, and she realised that by taking care of herself, she was better able to take care of her family.

### Take-home message:

*Prioritise self-care, even if it's just a few minutes a day. Your mental well-being benefits everyone in the family.*

## Daily Affirmations for a Thriving Mother

I am evolving every day.

My needs are valid.

I am more than what I do.

I permit myself to rest.

I am worthy of joy.

Write them. Say them aloud. Believe them.

### Final Thoughts

So if you're reading this, feeling lost or overwhelmed, here's what I want to tell you:

You haven't disappeared. You're transforming. Each diaper changed, each lullaby sung, each tear wiped — those are your new chapters. But the book is still yours to write.

Pick up the pen. Reclaim your name, your joys, your boundaries, your dreams.

Motherhood is a part of your identity. But it isn't your whole story

Reclaiming your identity beyond motherhood is not about going back to who you were — it's about discovering who you are now. You are still the woman who has passions, dreams, and a life outside of being a mother. It's okay to take time for yourself, nurture your relationships, and embrace the changes in your body and mind.

The "new you" is a beautiful evolution, and it's important to honour it. You are more than a mother — you are a woman, with a rich, full identity that deserves attention and care.

### Take-home message:

*Thriving is your birthright. Not just for your baby's sake—but for your own. Embrace the new version of yourself. You are still you — strong, beautiful, and capable — just with a little more love in your heart and wisdom in your soul.*

## Chapter - 11

# Stories from the Matriarchs - Wisdom from Mothers before Us – Real Stories, Cultural Insights, Interviews with Mothers of All Ages.

Every mother carries within her a story — one that holds wisdom, resilience, vulnerability, and strength. In this chapter, we share some heartfelt narratives from Indian mothers of different generations, reflecting the emotional truths, cultural nuances, and personal lessons that shaped their journeys. Each story brings alive what we've explored in earlier chapters — identity, support systems, mental health, self-care, and the invisible load of motherhood. I would like to share some stories that are close to me, but first I would like to talk about myself to make you feel that it's good to share and talk about your experiences.

## My First Days as a Mother – A Storm I Survived

The day my daughter was born, at 7:16 AM, I wasn't flooded with joy or swept away by that cinematic rush of emotions everyone talks about. I was waiting. Anxiously. Because moments after she arrived, she was rushed to the NICU. She was blue. Her oxygen levels weren't stabilising.

Usually, mothers are shown their babies soon after birth. But my husband, wanting to protect me from the sight of our baby in distress, made a decision — one I now understand but at that moment left me confused and aching. Everyone else in the family saw her from a distance. I waited. I was told, "She's fine. You'll see her soon."

That soon came only at 8:30 PM. My husband, who had stood by me all day, had to leave for a professional commitment. And so, I met my daughter for the first time not with him, but with our four parents. And despite all the fear and waiting, the moment was pure magic. A tiny bundle with curled fingers and my nose — she was mine.

But reality hits fast. I had read all about how to breastfeed, practised holding a pillow and toy in position— but when I held my real baby, I froze. How do I hold her without hurting her? How do I feed her? Thankfully, the nurses helped. My little warrior latched on beautifully. But the milk wasn't enough. She needed formula. And I needed to accept that.

That night, my mother and I noticed her breathing seemed off again. The nurse brushed off our concern. But I knew something wasn't right. "Mother's intuition," they call it. I insisted. I called my paediatrician friend and, acting on her advice, had my baby shifted back to the NICU. My husband, a pulmonologist, took one look and moved swiftly. Our baby was back on oxygen, and back into the ICU.

That was the first time I truly broke down.

I had a C-section. I could barely walk. But I begged the doctors to let me see her in the NICU. When they agreed, I went, heart in my throat, to sit by her side. That's when the next hurdle hit — pumping milk. I had all the equipment, the know-how. But nothing came. No one had told me that machine pumping doesn't work well in the first couple of days. I felt like a failure.

I kept hearing how vital the "first milk" is — and I couldn't give it.

It took my aunt, a paediatrician, physically showing me how to hand express colostrum. It helped a little. Until my milk came in, my daughter was fed donor milk from a hospital milk bank. That fact alone gave me so much peace — knowing that somewhere, another mother's generosity was helping my child survive.

Soon after, she was shifted to another NICU — across the road, at a hospital better equipped for her needs. I wasn't discharged yet. I couldn't even walk properly. I sent what little milk I could collect. But guilt crushed me. I didn't know how to ask for help or information. As a doctor myself, I felt I should know. But I didn't. If you're reading this, please remember: You're not supposed to know it all. Even if you're a doctor, a nurse, or someone who's helped a hundred others, when it's your own baby, it's different. You are not weak. You are just new to this. And it's okay to ask.

I didn't want to go home without my baby. So, with the support of my incredibly understanding husband and family, we stayed at a nearby hotel. I watched videos on YouTube, practised breast massage, tried everything possible. And finally — after 60 hours — my milk came in. That moment sparked something inside me. Hope. My husband's support and my mother's relentless care pulled me out of the dark fog I had sunk into.

Every night, we'd collect milk and walk to the NICU. Seeing my daughter — wires, oxygen masks, IV lines — it broke me anew every time. I had seen babies in this condition before during medical rounds. But this was my baby. And the pain was something no textbook could have prepared me for.

Eventually, after days of emotional highs and lows, our daughter was moved out of the ICU. We stayed with her. The paediatrician patiently answered all my doubts and reassured me. When we were finally discharged, we returned to a beautifully decorated home — thanks to my cousins. That moment was healing in ways I can't describe.

### Take-home message:

*Breast milk may not come immediately after birth. Especially after a C-section, hormonal shifts may take time. Don't blame yourself.*

Colostrum must be expressed manually. Pumping won't work initially — no one told me this.

Milk banks are a blessing. If you have excess supply, please consider donating.

Choose your hospital wisely. Ask about NICU availability, staff expertise, and emergency preparedness— not just the aesthetics.

Speak up. Don't be ashamed to ask questions, even if you think they're silly.

Support matters. A kind word, a helpful gesture, a presence — these can pull a mother back from the brink.

Decorate your home. That first entry with your baby will be etched in your memory forever.

Most importantly: IT'S OKAY. Whatever didn't go as planned — it's okay. Cry. Break down. But never blame yourself

To every new mother reading this: If your first few days felt anything like mine — overwhelming, scary, full of guilt and confusion — I want you to know, you're not alone. And no matter how tough the start is, you will get through this. You are stronger than you know. And your baby already thinks the world of you

## Story 1: Anjali – The Reluctant Return

Anjali, a marketing executive from Mumbai, had always been fiercely independent. She loved her job, thrived on deadlines, and took pride in her ability to multitask. But when her son, Kabir, was born, everything changed.

The first few months of maternity leave were a whirlwind of sleepless nights, feeding schedules, and endless diaper changes. Anjali adored Kabir, but she also felt like she was losing pieces of herself — the professional, the woman who once dreamed big.

As her leave neared its end, anxiety crept in. “I was excited to see my colleagues and get back to my work,” she confessed, “but I was also terrified of leaving Kabir. The guilt was crushing.”

Her husband, Rohit, was supportive but couldn’t fully grasp the depth of her emotions. “He said, ‘You’re doing great. You’re a supermom,” Anjali recalled, “but that didn’t erase the feeling that I was choosing work over my baby.”

The day Anjali returned to the office, she felt like a different person. She juggled pumping milk in a cramped, unfamiliar space, managed calls while calming Kabir over video, and fought waves of guilt and exhaustion.

She remembers one particular afternoon when she broke down in the restroom, overwhelmed by separation anxiety. A kind colleague, Neha, noticed and offered a listening ear.

“Neha told me, ‘You’re not alone in this. Many of us have been here. It’s okay to feel this way.’ That made a world of difference.”

Anjali began to create a pumping schedule, coordinated with Rohit to ensure Kabir was fed with expressed milk during the day, and found small moments to breathe — morning walks before work, a weekend coffee date with friends.

She also spoke openly with her manager about flexible hours and work-from-home days, carving out a rhythm that worked for her family.

"It wasn't easy," she said, "but over time, I rebuilt my confidence. I learned that returning to work doesn't mean losing yourself — it means evolving."

💡 Take-home message:

*Returning to work after maternity leave is emotionally complex. Prepare a plan for pumping and feeding, seek support from colleagues and family, and communicate your needs at work. Remember, it's okay to feel conflicted. With time and compassion, you can find balance and reclaim your identity.*

### Story 2: Lakshmi – The Breastfeeding Battle

Lakshmi, a young mother from Chennai, had imagined breastfeeding as the most natural and beautiful part of motherhood. She pictured quiet, tender moments nursing her newborn, feeling an unspoken bond deepen with each feed.

But reality was different.

From the very first latch, Lakshmi struggled. Her baby, Aarav, fussed and pulled away. Her nipples were sore, cracked, and bleeding. She felt exhausted and overwhelmed — torn between the instinct to feed and the pain that made her want to give up.

"People kept saying, 'Breastfeeding is natural; you just have to try harder,'" Lakshmi shared. "But no one talked about the difficulties, the pain, or the emotional toll."

Lakshmi's mother-in-law, though loving, added pressure. "Formula milk is for lazy mothers," she'd whisper, or "Why can't you feed properly like your sister-in-law?" Her words, meant to encourage, only deepened Lakshmi's guilt and shame.

After days of crying in silence, Lakshmi confided in her husband, Rajesh. He held her hands and said, "We will figure this out together. You are doing your best, and that's enough."

Together, they reached out to a lactation consultant recommended by a friend. The consultant helped Lakshmi understand Aarav's latch issues, taught her techniques like the football hold and breast compressions, and encouraged skin-to-skin contact to stimulate milk flow.

Lakshmi learned that pain was often due to improper latch or positioning — not her body failing her.

They also discussed the option of expressing milk using a pump. Lakshmi was hesitant, but the consultant explained how to store breast milk safely, labelling containers with date and time, and using refrigerated milk within 3 days or frozen milk within three months.

This flexibility gave Lakshmi some relief. On days when she was too tired or sore, Rajesh could feed Aarav with expressed milk, and sometimes, when necessary, formula was introduced without guilt.

Lakshmi's journey wasn't perfect, but it was hers — full of perseverance, learning, and support.

"I realised feeding my baby doesn't have to be all or nothing," she said. "Whether breast milk, formula, or donor milk, what matters most is love and nourishment."

**Take-home message:**

*Breastfeeding struggles are common and don't mean failure. Seek help early from lactation consultants or support groups. Remember, feeding your baby is a personal journey — whether breast milk, formula, or a mix. The most important thing is the bond you build, not the method you use.*

### Story 3: Nilofer – Breaking Generational Cycles

Nilofer, a software engineer from Hyderabad, had always admired her mother's strength. Raised in a traditional Muslim household, her mother, Ayesha, had given birth to five children with little rest and fewer complaints. "We didn't talk about feelings," Nilofer recalls. "Motherhood was duty, sacrifice, and silence."

When Nilofer became pregnant with her first child, she wanted something different. She wanted to embrace motherhood with openness and self-compassion. But the echoes of her mother's generation were loud.

During her pregnancy, Ayesha moved in to help. She was a fountain of practical wisdom — the best foods to eat, the rituals to follow, the importance of discipline. Yet, her advice often came with unspoken expectations: "You must do this because I did, and it's right."

Nilofer's husband, Imran, was supportive but often caught between his mother's traditional views and Nilofer's modern approach. After the baby's birth, tensions surfaced.

Nilofer wanted to rest, sleep when the baby slept, and accept help without guilt. Ayesha expected her to be up early, cooking and cleaning, believing "a hardworking mother is a good mother." When Nilofer expressed feelings of exhaustion and anxiety, Ayesha said, "You're too soft. We didn't have such luxuries."

It was a challenging phase. Nilofer felt torn — grateful for her mother's support but trapped by the weight of old beliefs.

One day, during a rare moment alone, Nilofer called her mother. She shared how she felt — the pressure, the fatigue, the sadness behind her smile.

To her surprise, Ayesha listened quietly.

Then she said, "Beta, I was also trapped in silence. I didn't know how to say no or ask for rest. I want you to have what I couldn't."

That conversation was a turning point. From then on, Ayesha tried to listen more and impose less. Nilofer found ways to include her mother's wisdom while setting boundaries for her own mental health.

Imran became a bridge, gently mediating when tensions flared, reminding everyone that motherhood is evolving.

Nilofer also joined a mothers' support group where women shared stories of generational expectations and new ways of parenting.

"I realised healing is not just about me," she said. "It's about changing the story for my child — and maybe for my mother too."

**❢ Take-home message:**

*Breaking generational cycles requires courage, honest communication, and empathy for both past and present. Honouring family wisdom while setting boundaries for your own wellbeing creates space for healing and growth. Remember, motherhood can be a bridge between tradition and change — your voice matters*

### *Story 4: Sunita – The Unseen Grief*

Sunita was the picture of joy during her pregnancy. Married at 27 and living in a bustling household in Jaipur, she was surrounded by family who eagerly awaited the arrival of her first child. Friends and relatives showered her with blessings, advice, and gifts. But behind her bright smile, Sunita carried a secret she hardly dared speak of.

After her son was born, everything seemed perfect. She had a healthy baby, a supportive husband, Rajesh, and loving in-laws. But beneath the surface, Sunita felt an overwhelming sadness that refused to lift.

"I thought it was just tiredness at first," she shared quietly. "But the sadness stayed. I couldn't explain it, and I felt guilty. Everyone said, 'You have a healthy baby, what are you sad about?' I felt like I was failing as a mother."

Sunita's days became a blur of feeding, diaper changes, and restless nights. She struggled to connect with her son in the way she imagined she would. Instead of joy, she felt numbness, and sometimes a deep ache in her chest she couldn't name.

Her husband Rajesh noticed the change but wasn't sure how to help. "I asked her what was wrong," he said. "She'd say, 'Nothing.' It was hard to watch someone you love suffer and not know how to fix it."

Sunita's mother-in-law, though well-meaning, dismissed her feelings. "You're just tired. Sleep more and you'll feel better," she advised, not realising the emotional storm raging inside her daughter-in-law.

For months, Sunita carried this invisible burden alone.

It wasn't until a routine postnatal checkup that her doctor gently asked, "How are you feeling emotionally? Are you having any thoughts that worry you?"

That question was a turning point.

Sunita opened up about her sadness and exhaustion, and her doctor diagnosed her with postpartum depression. She was relieved to finally have a name for her feelings and was started on counselling and mild medication.

Counselling helped Sunita process her grief and guilt. She learned that postpartum depression is common and nothing to be ashamed of. She found strength in sharing her story with a local mothers' support group, where others had faced similar struggles.

Her husband became her partner in healing — attending therapy sessions, helping with nighttime feeds, and offering constant reassurance. Slowly, Sunita began to feel herself returning, piece by piece.

Reflecting on her journey, she said, "The hardest part was feeling invisible. Like my pain didn't matter because I had a healthy baby. But my feelings mattered. Asking for help saved me."

**Take-home message:**

*Postpartum depression and emotional struggles are common but often hidden behind smiles and social expectations. Recognising symptoms, speaking openly, and seeking professional help can transform healing. Family support and understanding play a crucial role in recovery. Remember, your feelings are valid — you are not alone.*

### Story 5: Devika – Motherhood in Midlife

Devika was 38 when she held her newborn son in her arms for the first time. After years of career-building and navigating societal whispers about "the ticking clock," her journey to motherhood had been long and filled with hope and heartache. As a senior manager in a Mumbai-based company, she had just hit her professional stride when she found out she was pregnant.

The news was joyous, but it came with its own set of challenges.

Her body wasn't as quick to bounce back as she had imagined. Nights were harder; sleep didn't come easily, and aches lingered longer. Friends around her were already juggling toddlers and school runs, and some whispered about how "late" she was to motherhood.

Devika felt isolated. "I was expected to be grateful, but there was a secret loneliness," she said. "Being an older mother meant I had to battle my own energy levels and the assumptions of others."

Her husband, Sunil, was her rock — supportive and loving — but even he was learning as they went along. "He'd say, 'You look tired,' and I'd say, 'No, I feel tired.' There's a difference."

Devika's mother-in-law worried openly about her stamina, often comparing Devika to younger mothers in the neighbourhood. "You must rest more," she would say, sometimes in a tone that felt like an accusation.

Yet, Devika found strength in small rituals. She started meditation, something she'd always wanted to try but never found the time for. She joined a mothers' group online specifically for women over 35, where she found stories that mirrored her own — of fears, of joy, of exhaustion, and unexpected resilience.

Work was another puzzle. Returning to the office after maternity leave felt overwhelming. She negotiated flexible hours and remote work days, which her company accepted — a relief, but also a constant juggle.

One afternoon, during a particularly tough day, she confided in a colleague. "I feel like I'm doing double shifts — as a mom and as a manager. It's exhausting to prove I'm still capable in both roles."

Her colleague smiled gently. "You're not alone. Motherhood at any age is transformative. The trick is to redefine success, not replicate old versions of yourself."

That idea resonated deeply.

Devika began carving out time for herself, even if just fifteen minutes a day — reading, journaling, walking. She stopped comparing her experience to younger mothers and started celebrating her unique journey.

She also made peace with accepting help from family, friends, and hired support. "For a long time, I thought I had to do it all," she admitted. "Now I know strength is knowing when to lean on others."

Today, Devika's son is two, and she feels more centred, more confident. "Motherhood didn't come on my schedule," she said with a smile, "but it came with gifts I didn't expect — patience, deeper empathy, and a fiercer love than I knew I could hold.

Take-home message:

*Motherhood in midlife comes with unique physical, emotional, and social challenges. Embracing self-compassion, setting realistic expectations, and seeking supportive communities can transform the experience. Strength lies not in doing everything alone, but in knowing when to ask for help and adapt gracefully.*

## Story 6: Jaya – The Invisible Load

Jaya had always been the dependable one. Eldest of three sisters, she grew up in a small town in Tamil Nadu, where responsibility came early and praise was rare. When she married and moved to Chennai, she brought with her a deep-seated belief that love is shown through service — through clean homes, warm meals, and ticking off every task silently and perfectly.

When her daughter was born, the checklist only grew longer.

Wake up at 5 a.m., pump milk, prepare her husband's lunchbox, sterilise bottles, change diapers, rock the baby to sleep, bathe her, feed her, repeat. Her in-laws lived with them, and while they were kind, they expected the house to function like clockwork. Her husband, Rajiv, was well-meaning but absorbed in work. He often said, "Just tell me what to do, I'll help," not realising that the planning was part of the burden too.

"I was carrying a mental load no one could see," Jaya shared years later. "I was the project manager of our lives. Everyone followed instructions, but no one asked who was writing them."

She didn't even realise how heavy it had all become until one evening, she forgot to put salt in the sambar. Her mother-in-law casually commented, "You seem distracted these days." It was meant lightly, but something inside her cracked.

That night, Jaya sat on the floor of the kitchen and cried— not because of the salt, but because she felt utterly invisible. Her hands did everything, her mind remembered everything, but she felt like she was slowly disappearing into the walls of her home.

The next day, she wrote a long message to Rajiv while he was at work. She poured her heart out — the fatigue, the mental clutter, the pressure to keep everyone's life running while hers stood still. It wasn't angry. It was raw. Honest.

Rajiv came home early. For the first time, he asked, "What can we do to make this better?"

That week, they sat down and divided household responsibilities — not based on gender, but capacity. He began handling bedtime. He learned how to cook a couple of meals a week. They both started using a shared app to track the baby's needs and groceries. Jaya began to journal again, using mornings just for herself before the day began.

She also joined an online community called "Moms Who Delegate" and began attending short therapy sessions.

"I didn't want sympathy," she said. "I just wanted a partnership. I wanted to be seen."

Now, when her daughter is older and watches both parents working together at home, Jaya smiles. "We're raising her to believe that motherhood is not martyrdom. That her needs will always matter."

💡 Take-home message:

*The invisible load of motherhood includes all the unspoken planning, remembering, and emotional labour. It's okay to speak up. Asking for help isn't weakness — it's a radical step towards balance. When responsibilities are shared, so is the joy.*

### Story 7: Manju – Rediscovering Joy

Manju had always been the life of the party. A Kathak dancer by passion and a part-time art teacher in Pune, she radiated warmth and energy. But after the birth of her twins, everything about her identity seemed to slip through her fingers. She barely recognised herself.

"I used to wear bright colours, dance every morning. But after the delivery, all I wore were feeding gowns and had dark circles," she laughed, though her eyes misted as she spoke. "I was so wrapped in diapers and feeds that I forgot what happiness felt like."

Manju's postpartum period was tough. Both babies had colic, and her husband worked night shifts. Her mother-in-law was supportive, but often reminded her how her own days had been tougher — without diapers, formula, or domestic help. "We did it all, you can too," she'd say with a well-meaning smile that Manju had come to dread.

She reached a breaking point one evening, trying to soothe one twin while the other screamed, and her dinner went cold again. That night, she called her childhood friend Ritu, who had also become a mother recently.

"Ritu said something that stayed with me," Manju recalled. "'You don't have to do it all, M.' That sentence permitted me to pause. To breathe."

Slowly, Manju started carving out tiny bits of herself from the mess. She began dancing again — just ten minutes in the kitchen, with earphones in, swaying while the babies napped. She painted a small corner of her balcony in warm shades and called it her "five-minute café."

She also began journaling again — not long entries, just small lines like, "Today I made them smile," or "I'm tired, but I'm proud."

One Sunday, she left the babies with her mother-in-law and attended a local moms' meet. It felt strange at first, introducing herself as "just a mom." But as the conversations flowed, she found laughter again — shared stories, mutual frustration, collective healing.

"I wasn't alone. That changed everything," she said.

The turning point came when her husband surprised her with a registration for a weekend art workshop. "Go," he said. "I've got the kids." She cried — out of joy, gratitude, and the recognition that she was still seen.

Now her twins are four, and Manju teaches dance part-time. "I didn't bounce back," she says. "I evolved. And I'm proud of the woman I met in the mirror when I stopped trying to be perfect."

❢ Take-home message:

*Rediscovering joy after motherhood is not selfish — it's necessary. You don't need hours or grand plans. Sometimes, ten minutes of doing something that's just for you can help reconnect with who you were — and who you still are. Healing happens not when the chaos ends, but when we begin to find ourselves in the middle of it.*

### Story 8: Reena & Aarav – The Partner She Needed

Reena and Aarav had been married for four years before they decided to have a baby. It was a mutual decision, but like many Indian couples, the journey to parenthood was painted with expectations from their families. Reena was a school teacher from Bengaluru, and Aarav worked in IT. Their bond was solid, built on humour, shared playlists, and Friday night dosas. But nothing had prepared them for how much parenthood would reshape their relationship.

During pregnancy, Aarav accompanied Reena to every appointment. He read articles, joined a prenatal yoga class with her, and even took a short paternity prep course online. He was present, but Reena still felt alone in her changing body and mind.

"I remember crying one night because I felt ugly, stretched, and scared," Reena shared. "Aarav held my belly, kissed my forehead, and said, 'You are creating life. That's the most beautiful thing I've ever seen.'"

Post-delivery, the early days were fogged by sleep deprivation and endless feeding cycles. Aarav's office granted him two weeks of paternity leave, but as soon as he returned to work, Reena began to feel the weight of motherhood sink in. She was home all day, breastfeeding, struggling with a healing body and postpartum blues, while everyone else's life moved on.

One evening, she broke down. "I'm not coping, Aarav," she said. "I need more than diapers and dishes done. I need you to share this world with me, not just visit it."

Aarav listened. Really listened.

From that day, he began waking up for every second night feed, even if it was just to offer her a glass of water. He researched lactation support and helped Reena connect with a counsellor. They split chores not by tradition, but by energy. He started saying, "We're parents," instead of "You're the mom."

When relatives began offering unsolicited advice, he stood up for her. "This is Reena's recovery space," he once told his own mother gently when she criticised her for resting too much.

On weekends, he'd take their daughter out for walks so Reena could nap or write in her journal.

Years later, Reena reflects, "It wasn't grand gestures. It was consistency, empathy, and teamwork. Aarav didn't become a 'help' me parent. He became a parent."

**Take-home message:**

*The role of a supportive husband begins long before the baby is born. It involves emotional presence, equal participation, and defending space for the mother to heal and grow. True partnership in parenting is built in small, everyday acts of solidarity and love.*

These stories remind us that motherhood is never one-size-fits-all. It's layered with challenges, revelations, and small victories. As Indian mothers, we navigate not just parenting, but patriarchy, tradition, expectation, and healing.

You are not alone. And you're never too late to rewrite your story.

**Take-home message:**

*Trust your intuition, ask for help, honour your needs, and never forget—you are raising yourself alongside your child.*

## Chapter – 12

# A Letter to the New Mom - Gentle Words for the Hard Days

A Letter to the New Mom – Gentle Words for the Hard Days

Dear New Mom,

If you are holding this book in your hands, chances are you are walking through one of the most beautiful yet challenging phases of life — motherhood. I want to start by saying this: You are seen. You are heard. You are enough.

Motherhood is a paradox — joy and exhaustion, love and fear, strength and vulnerability all wrapped up in endless cycles of days and nights. Some days will feel like magic; others will feel like survival. And both are perfectly okay.

You may be overwhelmed, questioning every decision, and wondering if you're "doing it right." I want to reassure you that there is no one right way. Your journey is unique, shaped by your body, your baby, your family, and your heart.

In the pages before this, we talked about physical healing, emotional waves, relationships, identity, and rediscovering yourself. You have learned that asking for help is a strength, that your feelings are valid, and that self-care isn't selfish — it's essential.

Now, as you continue forward, here are some gentle reminders and practical tools to hold on to during the hard days.

### *Affirmations for the New Mom*

I am learning and growing every day.

My feelings are valid, even when they're complicated.

I am allowed to rest and ask for help.

My baby feels my love, even in moments of struggle.

I am more than my motherhood; I am a whole person.

It's okay to make mistakes; I am still enough.

This phase is temporary — I am strong enough to get through it.

## *Cheat Sheet: When to see a doctor*

| Area | What Helps | When to Seek Help |
|---|---|---|
| **Physical Recovery** | Gentle walking, balanced nutrition, pelvic floor exercises | If bleeding is heavy after 2 weeks, pain worsens, or the wound isn't healing |
| **Emotional Well-being** | Talk therapy, journaling, support groups | Persistent sadness, hopelessness, or thoughts of harming yourself or your baby |
| **Breastfeeding** | Lactation consultant, skin-to-skin contact | If the baby won't latch after several attempts or severe pain continues |
| **Support System** | Communicate needs, delegate chores | If you feel isolated or unsupported |
| **Work-Life Balance** | Flexible hours, pumping plans, and open dialogue with the employer | If work stress impacts mental health |

## Checklist: Daily Self-Care for You

Drink at least 8 glasses of water.

Eat nutrient-rich meals with protein, fruits, and vegetables.

Take 10 minutes to breathe deeply or meditate.

Move your body gently (stretch, walk, or yoga).

Connect with someone you trust (friend, partner, or support group).

Rest when baby rests—nap if you can

Journal or say out loud three things you are grateful for.

### *Chart: Sample Postpartum Routine (Flexible to Your Needs)*

| Time | Activity | Notes |
|---|---|---|
| **6:00 – 7:00 AM** | Morning walk or gentle stretches | Fresh air and movement energise |
| **7:00 – 8:00 AM** | Breakfast & feeding | Nourish yourself and baby |
| **8:00 – 10:00 AM** | Rest/nap while baby naps | Prioritize recovery |
| **10:00 – 12:00 PM** | Light chores or hobby time | Delegate household tasks |
| **12:00 – 1:00 PM** | Lunch | Balanced meal with protein |
| **1:00 – 3:00 PM** | Relaxation or connect with support | Call a friend or join a group |
| **3:00 – 5:00 PM** | Feeding and bonding | Skin-to-skin contact |
| **5:00 – 6:00 PM** | Prepare dinner or light activity | Involve family to share tasks |
| **6:00 – 7:00 PM** | Dinner | Family meal, nourishes everyone |
| **7:00 – 8:00 PM** | Wind down | Bath, reading, soft music |
| **8:00 PM onwards** | Sleep or rest | Prioritise sleep, seek help if needed |

### *Chart: Sharing the Load – Household Chores Distribution*

| Task | Mom's Role | Partner's Role | Family Help |
|---|---|---|---|
| **Cooking** | Meal planning | Help with prep | Family members can cook sometimes |
| **Cleaning** | Small daily tidying | Vacuuming, mopping | Rotate with siblings or parents |
| **Baby Care** | Feeding, changing | Night feeds, playtime | Grandparents babysitting occasionally |
| **Grocery Shopping** | List making | Shopping trips | Ask for deliveries when possible |
| **Emotional Support** | Express needs | Listen & encourage | Family check-ins and visits |

## *Final Thoughts from Me to You*

Motherhood is not a destination but a journey of rediscovery, growth, and resilience. Some days you will soar, others you will stumble. And both are part of the beautiful dance of life.

Be kind to yourself. Celebrate the small wins — the smile, the cuddle, the peaceful moment when your baby sleeps and you breathe a sigh of relief.

Remember, you are not alone. Reach out. Lean on your village. Your strength lies in your community as much as within you.

Above all, trust yourself. You know your baby best. You know your heart.

You are enough. You are loved. And you will get through these hard days.

With love and hope,

Dr. Shraddha Sanghani. A mother, a doctor and a fellow woman.

For any further help, you can reach me at www.drshraddhasanghani.com or email me at shraddhasanghanireddy@gmail.com.

Find me on Instagram under the handle drshraddhasanghani and follow for more.